T0146652

FRENCH FOR SUCCESS

PROGRESSIVE FRENCH GRAMMAR. BOOK 2
(INTERMEDIATE 1)

PHILIP EJIKEME

authorHOUSE®

AuthorHouse™ UK
1663 Liberty Drive
Bloomington, IN 47403 USA
www.authorhouse.co.uk
Phone: 0800.197.4150

Published by AuthorHouse 06/17/2016

ISBN: 978-1-5246-2927-4 (sc)
ISBN: 978-1-5246-2926-7 (e)

Print information available on the last page.

Contents

FOREWORD

FRENCH FOR SUCCESS is conceived to facilitate rapid mastery of the rules governing French grammar. It is the fruit of reflections on simple, but reliable methods that will enable the non-Francophone to acquire a mindset similar to that of the Francophone. To do that, we strive to simplify the conjugation of verbs, which is what makes the French language appear to be difficult. Accordingly, verbs are placed into categories, instead of groups, depending on their patterns of conjugation. Each category has a conjugation formula. A category is a group of verbs that share similar conjugation patterns in all tenses. While, traditionally, the radical of a verb is repeated six times in a conjugation, the concept exposed in these manuals seeks to use a radical once (unless it is impossible to do so, as in irregular verbs), and replace it with other radicals of the same category. As you will discover, verbs in the same categories share the same six endings which remain unchanged. Examples of radicals are: ***aim-*** from ***aimer***; ***parl*** from ***parler***, écout- from écouter or ***donn*** from ***donner***.

The groupings and their distinctive features are explained. Understanding that conjugation is just a matter of arrangement of verb endings, and knowing which verbs that belong together makes learning French much easier. Category A comprises over 4000 verbs, and one can learn their conjugation in less than 10 minutes.

The curious might wonder why we prefer categories to groups. Currently, there are three main groups namely the first group which comprises verbs ending in **er**; the second group which is composed of verbs ending in ***ir***; and the third group composed of verbs ending in ***re***. The first group alone (the ***er***-group) comprises about 13 different groups of verbs, the radicals of which cannot mutually replace one another. We reduce them to 8. For instance, ***donn-, aim-, parl-*** and écout- can replace one another but cannot replace céd-or cèd- from céder; or **jett** and **jet**- from **jeter**, etc, although they all end in er and belong to the first group.

In the second group, while ***fini- (finir), agi- (agir), and béni- (bénir)*** are mutually replaceable, they cannot replace **sor-(sortir), par-(partir), men-(mentir)**; cour-(courir), secour- (secourir); **or vien- and**

ven-(venir). We think that placing in the same group verbs whose patterns of conjugation have nothing to do with one another can lead to confusion.

Similarly, in group 3, which comprises verbs ending in re, while ***attendre, vendre, rendre, perdre*** can replace one another in a conjugation, they cannot replace ***prendre, comprendre***; and ***moudre, dissoudre*** and ***coudre*** do not even share common patterns of conjugation.

Themes are selected to facilitate visual recognition. Where possible, nouns, adjectives and adverbs are grouped in a manner that help the learner distinguish the gender and number, or show them how those parts of speech are formed.

The manuals are divided into four volumes for the progressive acquisition of the rules of French Grammar. While Book 1 introduces such basics as articles /gender (masculine/feminine), and nouns, prepositions, numbers, professions, book 2 seeks to consolidate the knowledge acquired earlier. Other tenses are examined in greater details.

Progressively, the users build their confidence as they learn to construct correct sentences.

Thank You/Remerciements

I wish to profoundly thank the following authors/publishers whose works I constantly consulted in the course of the preparation of these manuals:

Je tiens à exprimer mes vifs remerciements aux auteurs/éditeurs suivants dont les ouvrages m'ont été très utiles au cours de l'élaboration de ces manuels:

Maïa Grégoire and Odile Thiévenaz: Grammaire Progressive du Français avec 500 exercices CLE INTERNATIONAL, 1995, Paris.

Bescherelle POCHE : Les Tableaux pour conjuguer Les règles pour accorder Tous les verbs d'usage courant HATIER, Paris, Juin 1999

LE PETIT ROBERT 1 DICTIONNAIRE ALPHABÉTIQUE ET ANALOGIQUE DE LA

LANGUE FRANCAISE Paris, 1989

LE GRAND Robert & Collins Dictionnaire FRANÇAIS-ANGLAIS /ANGLAIS –FRANÇAIS

HarperCollins Publishers, 2007, Glasgow G64 2QT, Great Britain.

The AMERICAN HERITAGE dictionary of THE ENGLISH LANGUAGE, 3RD EDITION, 1992 Boston, MA 02116

I owe immense gratitude to Dr Varus SOSOE, who proofread the entire work. Thank you for your painstaking efforts.

Also to the migrant parents for whom I was occasionally invited to interpret by their children's schools in Geneva. Most often, those parents preferred to practice their French, allowing me to intervene only when they were in search of words. Whether they were Nigerians, Americans, British or Germans, the common features of their outputs had to do with verb endings that echoed the way it is done in their respective mother tongues. These manuals were conceived with a view to eliminating those errors. The desire to find a solution to the conjugation problems was partly born out of those encounters. I thank them for the inspiration.

Finally, I am grateful to my publishers, AuthorHouse UK, for the professionalism they displayed within a very short space of time.

Unit 1. Countries and nationalities; "en" as preposition for countries

En is a preposition of place. It is used before countries or states or locations, which, generally, are ***feminine, irrespective of whether they begin with a vowel or consonant.*** We use ***en*** to indicate a place where we are or live in, or to which we are travelling, if feminine.

Pays	***Masc/sing/pl***	***fem/sing/pl.***	***Countries***	***nationalities***
Albanie	albanais(s/p)	albanaise(s)	Albania	Albanian(s)
Afrique	africain(s)	africaine(s)	Africa	African(s)
Afrique du Sud	sud-africain(s)	sud-africaine(s)	S. Africa	South African(s)
Algérie	algérien(s)	algérienne(s)	Algeria	Algerian(s)
Allemagne	allemand(s)	allemand(s)	Germany	German(s)
Amérique	américain(s)	américaine(s)	America	American(s)
Andorre	andorran(s)	andorrane(s)	Andorra	Andoran(s)
Angleterre	anglais (s/pl.)	anglaise(s)	England	English
Argentine	argentin(s)	argentine(s)	Argentina	Argentinian(s)
Arménie	aménien(s)	arménienne(s)	Armenia	Armenian(s)
Asie	asiatique(s)	asiatique(s)	Asia	Asian(s)
Australie	australien(s)	australienne(s)	Australia	Australian(s)
Belgique	belge(s)	belge(s)	Belgium	Belgian(s)
Bolivie	bolivien(s)	bolivienne(s)	Bolivia	Bolivian(s)
Bosnie-Herzég.	bosnien(s)	bosnienne(s)	Bosnia-Herz.	Bosnian
	bosniaque(s)	bosniaque(s)		
Bulgarie	bulgarien(s)	bulgarienne(s)	Bulgaria	Bulgarian(s)
Chine	chinois (s/pl)	chinoise(s)	China	Chinese
Rép. Centrafricaine	centrafricain(s)	centrafricaine(s)	C.A.R	Central African(s)
Colombie	colombien(s)	colombienne(s)	Colombia	Colombian(s)
Corée du Nord/Sud	coréen(s)	coréenne(s)	Korea	Korean(s)
Côte d'Ivoire	ivoirien(s)	ivoirienne(s)	Ivory Coast	Ivorian(s)
Croatie	croate(s)	croate(s)	Croatia	Croatian(s)/Croat(s)
Rép. tchèque	tchèque(s)	tchèque(s)	Czech Rep.	Czech
Tchétchénie	tchétchène(s)	tchétchène(s)	Chechnya	Chechen(s)
Ecosse	ecossais	ecossaise(s)	Scotland	Scot(s)/Scottish
Egypte	égyptien(s)	égyptienne(s)	Egypt	Egyptian(s)
Espagne	espagnol(s)	espagnole(s)	Spain	Spanish/Spaniard
Gambie	gambien(s)	gambienne(s)	The Gambia	Gambian(s)
Guinée équatoriale	guinéen(s)	guinéenne(s)	Equat. Guinea	from E.Guinea
Erythrée	Érythréen(s)	érythréenne(s)	Eritrea	Eritrean(s)
Estonie	Estonien(s)	estonienne(s)	Estonia	Estonian(s)
Ethiopie	éthiopien(s)	éthiopienne(s)	Ethiopia	Ethiopian(s)

Europe	européen(s)	européenne(s)	Europe	European(s)
Finlande	finlandais	finlandaise(s)	Finland	Finn/Finnish
France	français	française(s)	France	French
Géorgie	géorgien(s)	géorgienne(s)	Georgia	Georgian(s)
Grèce	grec(s)	grècque(s)	Greece	Greek(s)
Grenade	grenadin(s)	grenadine(s)	Grenada	Grenadian(s)
Guinée	guinéen(s)	guinéenne(s)	Guinea	Guinean(s)
Hollande	hollandais	hollandaise(s)	Holland	Dutch
Hongrie	hongrois	hongroise(s)	Hungary	Hungarian(s)
Guyane	guyanais	guyanaise(s)	Guyana	Guyanese
Islande	islandais	islandaise(s)	Iceland	Icelandic/Icelander
Inde	indien(s)	indienne(s)	India	Indian(s)
Indonésie	indonésien(s)	indonésienne(s)	Indonesia	Indonesian
Irlande	irlandais	irlandaise(s)	Ireland	Irish
Italie	italien(s)	italienne(s)	Italy	Italian(s)
Jamaïque	jamaïcain(s)/ Jamaïquain(s)	jamaïcaine(s)/ jamaïquaine(s)	Jamaica	Jamaican(s)
Jordanie	jordanien(s)	jordanienne(s)	Jordan	Jordanian(s)
Lettonie	letton(s)	lettonne(s)	Latvia	Latvian
Libye	libyen(s)	libyenne(s)	Libya	Libyan(s)
Lithuanie	lithuanien(s)	lithuanienne(s)	Lithuania	Lithuanian(s)
Macédoine	macédonien(s)	macédonienne(s)	Macedonia	Macedonian(s)
Malaisie	malaisien(s)	malaisienne(s)	Malaysia	Malaysian(s)
Mauritanie	mauritanien(s)	mauritanienne(s)	Mauritania	Mauritanian(s)
Micronésie	micronésien(s)	micronésienne(s)	Micronesia	Micronesian(s)
Moldavie	moldave(s)	moldave(s)	Moldavia	Moldavian(s)
Mongolie	mongol(s)	mongole(s)	Mongolia	Mongol(s)/ Mongolian
Namibie	nambien(s)	namibienne(s)	Namibia	Namibian(s)
Nouvelle-Zelande	néo-zélandais	néo-zélandaise(s)	New Zealand	New Zealander
Norvège	norvégien(s)	norvégienne(s)	Norway	Norwegian
Papouasie-Nouv.G	papouan-néo-guinéen	papouan-néo-guinéenne	Papua New-Guinea	New-Guinean
Pologne	polonais	polonaise(s)	Poland	Polish/Pole(s)
Roumanie	roumain(s)	roumaine(s)	Romania	Romanian(s)
Russie	russe(s)	russe(s)	Russia	Russian(s)
Arabie Saoudite	saoudien(s)	saoudienne	Saudi Arabia	Saudi Arabian
Serbie	serbe(s)	serbe(s)	Serbia	Serbian(s)
Sierra Leone	sierra-léonien(s)	sierra-léonienne(s)	Sierra Leone	Sierra Leonian(s)

Slovaquie	slovaque(s)	slovaque(s)	Slovakia	Slovakian(s)
Slovénie	slovène(s)	slovène(s)	Slovenia	Slovenian(s)
Somalie	somalien(s)	somalienne(s)	Somalia	Somalian(s)
Suède	suédois	suédoise(s)	Sweden	Swedish/Swede(s)
Suisse	suisse(s)	suisse(s)	Switzerland	Swiss
Syrie	syrien(s)	syrienne(s)	Syria	Syrian(s)
Tanzanie	tanzanien(s)	tanzanienne(s)	Tanzania	Tanzanian(s)
Thaïlande	thaïlandais	thaïlandaise(s)	Thailand	Thai
Tunisie	tunisien(s)	tunisienne(s)	Tunisia	Tunisian(s)
Turquie	turc(s)	turque(s)	Turkey	Turk(s)/Turkish
Ukraine	ukrainien(s)	ukrainienne(s)	Ukraine	Ukrainian(s)
Zambie	zambien(s)	zambienne(s)	Zambia	Zambian(s)

These countries are feminine. So use ***en***:

Use en before these countries, which are feminine: En Allemagne, en Angleterre, en Afrique, en Albanie, en Côte d'Ivoire, en Chine, en Colombie, en Afrique du Sud, en Belgique.

En Allemagne, en Afrique du Sud, en Chine, en Ethiopie, en Guinée, en Indonésie, en Libye, en Pologne, en Angleterre, en France, en Colombie, en Argentine, en Côte d'Ivoire, en Belgique.

(in/to: Germany, South Africa, China, Ethiopia, Guinea, Indonesia, Libya, Poland, England, France, Colombia, Argentina, Ivory Coast, Belgium. Below are countries and their citizens.

Use "au" as preposition for masculine countries beginning with a consonant:
À + le = au; à + la = à la; à + l' = à l'; à + les = aux

Le Bangladesh, le Canada, le Bénin, le Soudan, etc.
Au Bangladesh, au Canada, au Bénin, au Soudan. – in /to Bangladesh, Canada, Benin, Sudan,

Use ***aux*** (plural) for countries composed of states or island countries composed of various islands:

Aux Etats-Unis, aux Pays-Bays, aux Philippines: (in/to : the United States, the Netherlands, hilippines).

Il habite ***aux*** Etat-Unis. – He lives in the United States.

Elles voyagent ***aux*** Etats-Unis – they are travelling to the United States.

Use **au** for these countries, which are all masculine: ***au*** Bangladesh, ***au*** Bénin, ***au*** Belize, etc.
Au:

Bangladesh	bangladais	bangladaise(s)	Bangladesh	Bangladeshi
Bélarus	bélarusse(s)	belarusse(s)	Belarus	Belarusian
Belize	belizien(s)	belizienne(s)	Belize	Belizean(s)

Bénin	béninois	béninoise(s)	Benin	Beninese
Bhoutan	bhoutanais	bhoutanaise(s)	Bhutan	Bhutanese
Botswana	botswanais	botswanaise(s)	Botswana	Batswana
Brésil	brésilien(s)	brésilienne(s)	Brazil	Brazilian(s)
Brunéi	brunéien(s)	brunéienne(s)	Brunei	from Brunei
Burkina Faso	Burkinabé	Burkinabé	Burkina Faso	fr. Burkina Faso
Burundi	burundais	burundaise(s)	Burundi	Burundian(s)
Cambodge	cambodgien(s)	cambodgienne(s)	Cambodia	Cambodian(s)
Cameroun	camerounais	camerounaise(s)	Cameroon	Cameroonian(s)
Canada	canadien(s)	canadienne(s)	Canada	Canadian(s)
Cap-Vert	cap-verdien(s)	cap-verdienne(s)	Cape Verde	Cape Verdean(s)
Tchad	tchadien(s)	tchadienne(s)	Chad	Chadian(s)
Chilli	chilien(s)	chilienne(s)	Chile	Chilean(s)
Congo	congolais	congolaise(s)	Congo	Congolese
Costa Rica	costaricain(s)/ costaricien(s)	costaricaine(s)/ costaricienne(s)	Costa Rica	Costarican(s)
Danemark	danois	danoise(s)	Denmark	Danish/Dane(s)
Etats-Unis	américain(s)	américaine(s)	United States	American(s)
Salvador	salvadorien(s)	salvadorienne(s)	El Salvador	Salvadorian(s) Salvadorean/ran
Gabon	gabonais	gabonaise(s)	Gabon	Gabonese
Ghana	ghanéen(s)	ghanéenne(s)	Ghana	Ghanaian(s)
Guatemala	guatémaltèque(s)	guatémaltèque(s)	Guatemala	Guatemalan(s)
Honduras	hondurien(s)	hondurienne(s)	Honduras	Honduran(s)
Japon	japonais	japonaise(s)	Japan	Japanese
Kazakhstan	**K**azakh(s)	kazakhe(s)	Kazakhstan	Kazakh(s)
Kenya	kényan(s)	kényane(s)	Kenya	Kenyan(s)
Kirghizistan	kirghiz	kirghiz	Kirghizstan	Kirghiz
Koweït	koweïtien(s)	koweïtienne(s)	Kuwait	Kuwaiti
Laos	laotien(s)	laotienne(s)	Laos	Laotian(s)
Lesotho	lesothans	lesothane(s)	Lesotho	Lesothan(s)/ Basotho
Liban	libanais	libanaise(s)	Lebanon	Lebanese
Libéria	libérien(s)	libérienne(s)	Liberia	Liberian(s)
Liechtenstein	Liechtensteinois	Liechtensteinoise(s)	Liechtenstein	fr. Liechtenstein
Luxembourg	luxembourgeois	luxembourgeoise(s)	Luxemburg	Luxemburger
Malawi	malawien(s)	malawienne(s)	Malawi	Malawian(s)
Mali	malien(s)	malienne(s)	Mali	Malian(s)
Maroc	marocain(s)	marocaine(s)	Morocco	Moroccan(s)

Mexique	mexicain(s)	mexicaine(s)	Mexico	Mexican(s)
Monténégro	monténégrin(s)	monténégrine(s)	Montenegro	Montenegrin(s)
Mozambique	mozambicain(s)	mozambicaine(s)	Mozambique	Mozambican(s)
Népal	népalais	népalaise(s)	Nepal	Nepalese/Nepali
Nicaragua	nicaraguayen(s)	nicaraguayenne(s)	Nicaragua	Nicaraguan(s)
Niger	nigérien(s)	nigérienne(s)	Niger	from Niger
Nigeria	nigérian(s)	nigériane(s)	Nigeria	Nigerian(s)
Pakistan	pakistanais	pakistanaise(s)	Pakistan	Pakistani
Panama	panaméen(s)	panaméenne(s)	Panama	Panamanian(s)
Paraguay	paraguayen(s)	paraguayenne(s)	Paraguay	Paraguayan(s)
Pays-Bas	hollandais	hollandaise(s)	The Netherlands	Dutch
Pérou	péruvien(s)	péruvienne(s)	Peru	Peruvian(s)
Portugal	portugais	portugaise(s)	Portugal	Portuguese
Qatar	qatari(s)	qatarie(s)	Qatar	Qatari(s)
Royaume-Uni	britannique(s)	britannique(s)	UK	British
Rwanda	rwandais	rwandaise(s)	Rwanda	Rwandan(s)
Sénégal	sénégalais	sénégalaise(s)	Senegal	Senegalese
Soudan	soudanais	soudanaise(s)	Sudan	Sudanese
Sri Lanka	sri-lankais	sri-lankaise(s)	Sri Lanka	Sri Lankan(s)
Surinam	surinamais	surinamaise(s)	Surinam	Surinamese
Swaziland	swazi(s)	swazie(s)	Swaziland	Swazi
Tadjikistan	tadjik(s)	tadjik(s)	Tadzhikistan	Tadzhik, Tajik
Togo	togolais	togolaise(s)	Togo	Togolese
Venezuela	vénézuélien(s)	vénézuélienne(s)	Venezuela	Venezuelan(s)
Vietnam	vietnamien(s)	vietnamienne(s)	Vietnam	Vietnamese
Yémen	yéménite(s)	yéménite(s)	Yemen	Yemenite(s)
Zimbabwe	zimbabwéen(s)	zimbabwéenne(s)	Zimbabwe	Zimbabwean(s)

***Use en also for masculine countries beginning with a vowel*:**

En

Afghanistan	afghan(s)	afghane(s)	Afghanistan	Afghan(s)
Angola	angolais	angolaise(s)	Angola	Angolan(s)
Azerbaïdjan	azerbaïdjanais	azerbaïdjanaise(s)	Azerbaijan	Azerbaijani/Azeri
Equateur	équatorien(s)	équatorienne(s)	Ecuador	Ecuadorian(s)/
	Ecuadoran(s)			
Haïti	Haïtien(s)	haïtienne(s)	Haiti	Haitian(s)
Irak	irakien(s)	irakienne(s)	Iraq	Iraqi(s)
Iran	iranien(s)	iranienne(s)	Iran	Iranian(s)
Israël	israélien(s)	israélienne(s)	Israel	Israeli(s)
Ouganda	ougandais	ougandaise(s)	Uganda	Ugandan(s)

Uruguay	uruguayen(s)	uruguayenne(s)	Uruguay	Uruguayan(s)
Ouzbékistan	ouzbek(s)	ouzbèke(s)	Uzbekistan	Uzbek(s)

En Iran, Irak, en Afghanistan, en Angola, en Equateur, en Haïti, en Ouganda, en Ouzbékistan, en Uruguay, en Israël.

For island countries, use **à** if masculine singular, **à la** if feminine singular, **aux** if plural; some, such as Trinité et Tobago, use **à** irrespective of being feminine

À Cuba, ***à*** Djibouti, à Fidji/aux Fidji, à Madagascar, à Maurice, à Malte, à Monaco, à Oman, à Singapour, à Sao Tomé et Principe, à Trinité et Tobago

In/to Cuba, Djibouti, Fiji, Madagascar, the Bahamas, the Seychelles, the Kiribati, the Comoros, Barbados, Grenada

à la Barbade, à la Grenade

aux Bahamas, aux Comores, aux Seychelles, aux Philippines, aux Kiribati

Bahamas	bahaméen(s)	bahaméenne(s)	The Bahamas	Bahamian(s)
Barbade	barbadien(s)	barbadienne(s)	Barbados	Barbadian(s)
Comores	comorien(s)	comorienne(s)	The Comoros	from the Comoros
Cuba	cubain(s)	cubaine(s)	Cuba	Cuban(s)
Djibouti	djiboutien(s)	djiboutienne(s)	Djibouti	from Djibouti
Grenade	grenadien(s)	grenadienne(s)	Grenada	Grenadian(s)
Kiribati	kiribati/gilbertin(s)	kiribati/gilbertine(s)	Kiribati	from the Kiribati
Madagascar	malgache(s)	malgache(s)	Madagascar	Madagascan(s)
Malte	maltais	maltaise(s)	Malta	Maltese
Maurice	mauricien(s)	mauricienne(s)	Mauritius	Mauritian(s)
Oman	omanais	omanaise(s)	Oman	Omani
Seychelles	seychellois	seychelloise(s)	Seychelles	from the Seychelles
Sao Tomé / Principe	saotomien(s)	saotomienne(s)	Sao Tomé	from Sao Tomé e Principe
Singapour	singapourien(s)	Singapouriennes(s)	Singapore	Singaporean(s)
Trinité et Tobago	trinidadien(s)	trinidadienne(s)	Trinidad &T.	Trinidadian(s)

For cities, use à (at/in)

À Abuja, à Enugu, à Owerri, à Paris, à Genève, à Zurich, à Londres, à Lagos, à Yaoundé, à Lomé, à Lisbonne, à Madrid, Pékin, à Christchurch, à Kingston, à Accra, à Libreville, à New York, à Washington, à Sao Paulo, à Conakry, à Libreville, à Bagdad, à Beyrouth, à Lima, à Caracas, à Tokyo, à Séoul, à Montréal, Tripoli, Dakar, à Tunis, à Casablanca, à Rabat, Moscou, à Abuja,

Note: La Californie = en Californie,
La Havane = à La Havane
Le Québec = au Québec, Le Caire = au Caire (in Cairo)
A la Mecque - in Mecca

Exercise 1.1. Put en, au, aux, à, à la

a. Mary Rogers habite______Canada, mais travaille______Etats-Unis

b. Birgit part samedi__________Allemagne.

c. Elle va______Berlin,______ Paris et__________Californie

d. Il y a 36 Etats______Nigeria. Mes frères habitent et travaillent______Lagos

e. Nous allons lundi_____ Enugu

f. Owusu Ansa habite.____Kumasi_____Ghana.

g. Vous aimeriez voyager______Oman ?

h. Mon patron part pour 2 mois______Barbade,___ Brésil, et___ Argentine.

i. Tundé Hounsou habite______Cotonou_________Bénin.

j. Est-ce que vous allez faire escale_____Amsterdam________Pays-Bas ?

k. On trouve ces produits______Moyen-Orient :_____Israël,_____Koweit,______Iran, Arabie Saoudite et______Yémen.

Exercise 1.2 Say their nationalities

a. E.g. Chike Okoro vient du Nigeria. Il est nigérian. Yetunde Dayo est nigériane.

b. Samuel Eto'o vient du Cameroun. Il est ________________. Mélanie et Gisèle Song viennent du Cameroun. Elles sont ______________________________________.

c. Tom vient des Etats-Unis d'Amérique. Il est____

d. Kumayo vient d'Afrique du Sud. Il est____

e. Consuelo travaille et vit à Caracas, au Venezuela. Elle est__________________________________

f. Estéban vit à La Havane à Cuba. Il est____

g. Annette habite à Paris, en France. Elle et ses amies sont____________________________________

h. Ses étudiantes viennent de Côte d'Ivoire. Elles sont___________________________________

i. Idriss vit et travaille en Libye, mais il n'est pas______________________________________

j. Anita vient d'Angleterre. Elle est____

k. Monsieur Fernandez, êtes-vous_______________(Pérou) ?

l. Li Na est______________Elle vient de Chine,

m. Est-ce que Renata est_____________(Allemagne) ou_____________(Autriche)

n. Lucie vient du Tchad. Elle est.____

o. Adama et Keita viennent de Guinée. Ils sont_______________________________________

p. Elena et Vladimir vivent à Moscou. Ils sont_____________(Russie).

q. Roger Federer est______________(Suisse).

r. Ces femmes sont______________(Éthiopie).

s. Cristiano Ronaldo est un joueur______________(Portugal)

t. Est-ce que vous êtes______________,______________ou_________________________________
(Iran, Irak, Afghanistan)

u. L'entraîneur est___________(Maroc) ; sa femme est________________(Tunisie)

Exercise 1.3 Use the information furnished to write the nationalities of the people below

E.g. Lucy et David (Angleterre). Lucy et David sont__________________________

a. Flavia et Roberta (Italie). Flavia et Roberta sont____________________________

b. Ronke est________Chika et Ronke sont__________________________(Nigeria)

c. Kwame et Rita (Ghana). Kwame est ghanéen. Rita est______________________

d. Noura et Samira sont____Tunisie)

e. Wolfgang est____________Renata est____________________________Allemagne)

f. Nadia est russe. Boris est________Boris et Nadia sont________________(Russie).

g. Julia Robert et Angelina Jolie sont des actrices___________________Amérique)

h. Nelly vient de la Barbade. Elle est__________John-Paul et Nelly sont_________

i. Usain Bolt et Johann Blake sont________________________________(Jamaïque)

j. Gaston Hounsou vient du Bénin. Il est__________________________________

k. Voici l'actrice______________________(Egypte)

l. Je vous présente le prince__________________(Arabie Saudite)

m. Nous avons rencontré le président________________(Oman)

Exercise 1.4 Form the plural of these nationalities.

Exemples: John et Christina: l'Amérique/Les Etats-Unis. – John et Christina sont américains
Dora et Céline: le Canada. – Dora et Céline sont canadiennes.

a. Youssef et Tariq: l'Egypte. -____________________________________

b. Louise et Catherine: les Seychelles. -______________________________

c. Justine et Daniel: la Belgique. -__________________________________

d. Adrianna et Cristina: le Brésil. -_________________________________

e. Jacques et Abdou: le Bénin. -____________________________________

f. Mary et Amina: le Nigeria.-_____________________________________

g. Toure et Camara: la Guinée. -____________________________________

h. Lévi et Obéd. L'Israél. -____

i. Gabriel et Isabelle sont. -_________________________________(Bénin)

Exercise 1.5 Observe agreement where necessary

Nokia est une marque finlandais***e***

a. Au Sushi Chef, on mange des spécialités japonais____

b. Le Futa Djallon est une épicerie guinéen____

c. Au Bollywood Flavour, on mange les spécialités indien____

d. Le gruyère et l'appenzellois sont des fromages suisse___

e. Au Moumounia, on mange les plats marocain___

f. Samsung et Daewoo sont des marques coréen___

g. Star et Gulder sont des boissons nigérian___

h. Boeing est un constructeur américain___

i. Est-ce qu'Airbus est une marque canadien_____ou européen_____?

Unit 2. Adjectives – agreement, position and function

It has been stated earlier that in French, adjectives agree in number and gender with the nouns, pronouns or the expression they qualify or describe. In other words, if the noun/pronoun is masculine and singular, the adjective will also be masculine/singular; similarly, if the noun/pronoun is fem/singular, the adjective will also be fem/singular. In French, unlike in English, adjectives take plural forms if the nouns/pronouns they relate to are in plural.

Generally, the ***feminine*** of an adjective is formed by adding an ***e*** to the masculine, as shown below. Correspondingly, the plural is formed by adding ***s*** to the masculine or feminine.
However, many adjectives do not follow this rule. (Other categories of adjectives will be treated later).

Masc/singular	***Fem/singular***
Jacques est un ***grand*** garçon	Nadia est une ***grande*** fille
Ikenna a un ***petit*** sac	Ada a une ***petite*** maison
Un vent ***fort*** (a strong wind)	Une boisson ***forte*** (a strong drink)
Masc/pl	***Fem/plural***
Michel et Pierre sont ***grands***	Sara et Nadia sont ***grandes***
Des piments fort***s***	Des épices ***fortes*** (strong spices)
Voici les ***petits*** frères de Yussef	Nuria a deux ***petites*** sœurs

When a plural case involves a combination of masculine and feminine singular or plural, the adjective is masculine plural:

Jacques et Sandra sont ***grands*** – Jacques and Sandra are tall

Masc/sing.	Masc/pl.	Fem/sing.	Fem/pl-	English
Intelligent	intelligents	intelligent***e***	intelligentes	intelligent
Joli	jolis	joli***e***	jolies	pretty
Poli	polis	poli***e***	polies	polite, polished
Malpoli	malpolis	malpoli***e***	malpolies	impolite, rude
Court	courts	court***e***	courtes	short
Vert	verts	vert***e***	vertes	green

Clair	clairs	clair***e***	claires	clear/bright
Gagnant	gagnants	gagnant***e***	gagnantes	winning
Gai	gais	gai***e***	gaies	cheerful, happy
Différent	différents	différent***e***	différentes	different
Gênant	gênants	gênant***e***	gênantes	irritating/awkward
Chaud	chauds	chaud***e***	chaudes	hot
Froid	froids	froid***e***	froides	cold
Laid	laids	laid***e***	laides	ugly
Présent	présents	présent***e***	présentes	present
Lourd	lourds	lourd***e***	lourdes	heavy
Haut	hauts	haut***e***	hautes	high
Puissant	puissants	puissant***e***	puissantes	powerful
Seul	seuls	seul***e***	seules	alone/lonely
Serein	sereins	serein***e***	sereines	calm
Sain	sains	sain***e***	saines	sound
Malsain	malsains	malsain***e***	malsaines	unhealthy, nasty, bad
Mondain	mondains	mondain***e***	mondaines	fashionable/ socialite
Vain	vains	vaine	vaines	vain/futile
Hautain	hautains	hautain***e***	hautaines	haughty, disdainful
Cohérent	cohérents	cohérent***e***	cohérentes	coherent
Étroit	étroits	étroit***e***	étroites	narrow
Pur	purs	pur***e***	pures	pure
Dur	durs	dur***e***	dures	hard, stiff, tough
Mûr	mûrs	mûr***e***	mûres	ripe, mature
Sûr	sûrs	sûr***e***	sûres	sure, certain

Position of adjectives:

While some adjectives are placed before the nouns they qualify, others are placed after the nouns. There are no rules indicating which adjectives are placed before or after the nouns they relate to. While in some cases, the position of the adjectives may not change the meaning of a noun, in other instances, the meaning changes. Even the same adjective can be placed before a noun to mean one thing; and after a noun to mean a different thing.

E.g: ***Prochain: before the nouns***:
Masculine: le prochain président - the next president, le prochain numéro – the next issue

Feminine: la prochaine directrice – the next principal/director, la prochaine fois – the next time ; la prochaine réunion – the next meeting etc.

Prochain – after the nouns: masculine: le mois prochain – next month, vendredi prochain, Feminine: la semaine prochaine, l'année prochaine, la prochaine fête

Un seul garçon – only one boy (not two)
Un garçon seul – a lonely boy
Une seule fille; une seule personne. (One girl, one person)
Une fille seule, une personne seule. (A lonely girl, a lonely person)

So, study and memorise the position of the adjectives in relation to a given noun.

Un joli cadeau	- a nice present;	une jolie fille – a pretty girl
Un homme poli	– a polite man;	une infirmière polie – a polite nurse
		une enseignante polie – a polite teacher

Des élèves polis – polite school children; des étudiantes polies – polite (female) students

Exercise 2.1 Choose the correct positions of the adjectives

a. Selon la météo, il va pleuvoir lundi prochain/prochain lundi.

b. Ma prochaine voiture/ma voiture prochaine sera une jeep.

c. Jacques aura 10 ans l'année prochaine/la prochaine année.

d. La tâche est énorme. Un seul garçon/garçon seul ne pourra pas faire ce travail.

e. Ma vie privée/privée vie ne regarde personne.

f. C'est un joli cadeau/cadeau joli.

g. C'est une haute montagne/montagne haute.

h. Ce sont des bus bleus/de bleus bus.

i. C'est une porte étroite/étroite porte.

j. L'entreprise américaine/américaine entreprise emploie 3000 personnes.

k. Les programmes suivants/suivants programmes s'adressent aux filles.

l. Un grand merci/merci grand à nos clients.

Exercise 2.2 Complete the sentences with the correct forms of the adjectives

E.g. Ces valises sont très____________________lourd

Ces valises sont très lourdes

a. Cette année, les jupes court_______sont à la mode

b. Ses propos sont cohérent_______, mais ses réponses ne sont pas cohérent_______.

c. En hiver, notre organisation distribue des repas chaud_______et des boissons chaud________

d. Seules les personnes présent_______peuvent voter.

e. Cette phrase n'est pas très clair_______

f. Envoyez-nous un courrier à l'adresse suivant_______

g. Mais tu as les mains froid__________

h. L'eau chaud________ sera coupée demain matin.

Unit 3. Adjectives ending in "e": grave, simple, digne, légitime, etc.

The masculine and feminine of such adjectives have the same form. Add "s" to form their plural

Singular (masc/fem)	plural (masc/fem)
Simple – un homme simple/une femme simple	Des hommes/des femmes simples
Jeune – un jeune homme, une jeune femme A young man, a young woman	De jeunes hommes, de jeunes femmes Young men, young women

Grave(s) une blessure grave - a serious wound; des blessures graves – serious wounds, injuries, son état (masc) est jugé grave. – His situation is serious

Sobre(s) – un homme sobre, une femme sobre - a sober man, a sober woman

Austère(s) – une vie austère, un moine austère - an austere life,

Sage – s***ages*** - un médecin sage; une sage-femme sage a wise doctor, a wise nurse

Malade(s) – un malade, une malade - a sick man, a sick woman

Connexe – connexes - un problème connexe, questions connexes – a related problem, related matters

Perplexe - Perplexes - baffled, puzzled

Digne - dignes - un travail digne, un salaire digne; une attitude digne – a fitting work, salary, attitude

Légitime(s) – légitimes - legitimate, lawful, justifiable

Leste – lestes: agile, nimble, supple

Manifeste manifestes - obvious, clear, evident; des cas manifestes de fraude – clear cases of fraud

Optimiste – optimistes – optimistic

Pessimiste – pessimistes – pessimistic

Tenace – tenaces - tenacious

Adjectives ending in –ble

Adorable(s), admirable(s), aimable(s) capable(s), confortable(s), durable(s), remarquable(s), fiable(s), responsable(s), indestructible(s), indésirable(s), indélébile(s), semblable(s), sensible(s), inoxydable(s), inoubliable(s), incollable(s), sociable(s) – les animaux sociables, impitoyable(s) – (un commerçant impitoyable), faible(s), inévitable(s)

Incollable – unbeatable, not sticky
Un joueur incollable, une danseuse incollable; des joueurs incollables

Un étudiant admirable, une femme admirable, des femmes admirables, des étudiants admirables.

Un bébé adorable, une princesse adorable

Un système fiable, une marque fiable – des systèmes fiables, des produits, des marques fiables

-que
Identique(s), pratique(s), britannique(s), épileptique(s), catastrophique(s), dramatique(s), le conseil catholique, la conférence islamique, un exercise physique, programme artistique, un bénéfice réciproque, une aide réciproque; un directeur/directrice dynamique, l'assistance juridique, l'agriculture biologique; un fantastique cadeau, une fantastique comédienne, un magnifique but, une magnifique robe
Fatidique – une décision fatidique (a crucial decision),
Le moment fatidique, l'heure fatidique – fateful moment/time, le jour fatidique – doomsday

-aire
Scolaire(s) –le programme scolaire, la cuisine scolaire; les programmes scolaires, les vacances scolaires

Similaire(s) – un problème similaire; une activité similaire; des questions similaires, des produits similaires

- Sommaire(s) – l'exécution sommaire, un programme sommaire, une audition sommaire

- élémentaire(s), rudimentaire(s), polaire(s), primaire(s), solitaire(s), spectaculaire(s)

- populaire(s), une chanson populaire, des manifestations populaires, des votations populaires, des fronts populaires, la démocratie populaire, le mot populaire

- Secondaire(s): (un personnage, le plan, le secteur secondaire; les effets secondaires, les activités secondaires)

- Séculaire(s) (tous les 100 ans), (arbre, haine)

- Sectaire(s) (une attitude, un comportement, une dérive sectaire, un indice, une appartenance, n caractère sectaire)

- ***Insulaire(s) (pays, villes, le peuple)*** - insular countries, cities, isolated people.

- ***interbancaire(s) (taux d'escompte, transactions)***

- ***solidaire(s), consulaire(s)***

- ***une société égalitaire***
- ***une mission suicidaire (tendances, idées suicidaires)***
- ***solaire (énergies, crème)***
- ***horaire (salaire horaire, décalage horaire, vitesse horaire***
- ***temporaire(s) (travail),***
- ***hebdomadaire(s) – weekly: parution, publication, salaire, journal, culte, réunions hebdomadaires***

Dentaire – la prothèse dentaire, le soin dentaire, les soins dentaires,

Moléculaire(s)- la biologie moléculaire

Autoritaire(s) – un président autoritaire, une directrice autoritaire, des parents autoritaires

Militaire(s) – une action/source militaire, un avion militaire;

Alimentaire(s) – le produit alimentaire – food ; la chaine alimentaire – food chain, la pension alimentaire – alimony, feeding/maintenance allowance, les denrées alimentaires/les produits alimentaires - foodstuff

Oculaire(s) – le globe oculaire – the eyeball, le témoin oculaire – the eyewitness

-gue: Analogue(s)

-ore: Incolore(s), inodore(s), sonore(s) (bip),

-ide, -ste: Avide(s), cupide(s), intrépide(s), rapide(s), rigide(s), stupide(s), torpide(s) (lésion, plaie), torride(s) (chaleur, climat), lucide(s) (rêve), robuste(s)

-ile : agile(s), fragile(s), débile(s), stérile(s), fertile(s), infertile(s), futile(s), utile(s), inutile(s), habile(s) – un homme habile, une femme habile; des étudiants habiles;
tactile(s) – un écran tactile ; mobile(s) – une pièce mobile, une échelle mobile, un radar mobile ; hostile(s) – un accueil hostile, une réaction hostile, un climat hostile

-ole: frivole(s), drôle(s),
-ace : loquace(s) – un homme ou une femme loquace – (talkative) ; sagace(s), perspicace(s), efficace(s), inefficace(s)

Masculine adjectives in -er, the feminines in ère

Masc/sing	***masc.plural***	***Fem./sing.***	***Fem./plural***	***English***
-er	***-ers***	***-ère***	***-ères***	
Léger	légers	légère	légères	light
Financier	financiers	financière	financières	financial
Frontalier	frontaliers	frontalière	frontalières	border/frontier
Transfrontalier	transfrontaliers	transfrontalière	transfrontalières	cross-border
Cher	chers	chère	chères	dear/expensive/costly
Immobilier	immobiliers	immobilière	immobilières	real-estate, property
Fier	fiers	fière	fières	proud
Foncier	fonciers	foncière	foncières	property/land/ed
Princier	princiers	princière	princières	princely
Dernier	derniers	dernière	dernières	last
Premier	premiers	première	premières	first
Hospitalier	hospitaliers	hospitalière	hospitalières	hospital-related
Inhospitalier	inhospitaliers	inhospitalière	inhospitalière	harsh, inhospitable
Hôtelier	hôteliers	hôtelière	hôtelières	hotel, hotel-related
Régulier	réguliers	régulière	régulières	regular,
Particulier	particuliers	particulière	particulière	individual, particular, special, specific

Other Adjectives: Masculine in -et Feminine in ète

Masc/sing.	***Masc/plural***	***Fem/sing***	***Fem/plural***	***English***
-et	***-ets***	***-ète***	***-ètes***	
Discret	discrets	discrète	discrètes	discreet/reserved
Concret	concrets	concrète	concrètes	concrete/real/practical
Secret	secrets	secrète	secrètes	secret

Other adjectives and their gender forms

If the masculine of the adjective ends in "el", the feminine will be "-elle"

Masc/singular	***Masc/pl.***	***Fem/sing***	***Fem/pl***	***English***
-el	***-els***	***-elle***	***-elles***	
- actuel	actuels	actuelle	actuelles	current
- personnel	personnels	personnelle	personnelles	personal

- professionnel	professionnels	professionnelle	professionnelles	professional
- sensationnel	sensationnels	sensationnelle	sensationnelles	sensational
- occasionnel	occasionnels	occasionnelle	occasionnelles	occasional
- officiel	officiels	officielle	officielles	official
- matériel	matériels	matérielle	matérielles	material
- spirituel	spirituels	spirituelle	spirituelles	spiritual
- ponctuel	ponctuels	ponctuelle	ponctuelles	punctual/isolated
- culturel	culturels	culturelle	culturelles	cultural
- mutuel	mutuels	mutuelle	mutuelles	mutual
- interculturel	interculturels	interculturelle	interculturelles	intercultural
- multiculturel	multiculturels	multiculturelle	multiculturelles	multicultural
- présidentiel	présidentiels	présidentielle	présidentielles	presidential

Le président actuel – the current president; la directrice actuelle – the current director/headteacher
- personnel – le code personnel – personal code; les données personnelles – personal data

Exercise 3.1 ***Complete the sentences with the correct forms of the adjectives, respecting gender and number (masculine/feminine; singular/plural).***

E.g. Voici ta carte d'accès____________________.(personnel)
Voici ta carte d'accès personnelle.

a. Entrez votre code____________________(personnel)

b. Parlez-nous de vos défis_______________.(professionnel)

c. Pour ce poste, on demande 5 ans d'expérience__________________.(professionnel).

d. Cette semaine, nous avons des actions__________(sensationnel) dans notre magasin.

e. Certaines entreprises interdisent les e-mails non professionnel______au travail.

f. Les prix_____________(actuel) sont intéressants.

g. Voici nos offres (promotionnel_______) pour la saison d'hiver.

h. Je n'ai pas son adresse (officiel)__________

i. Ils ont besoin de l'aide matériel________et du soutien spirituel________

j. Il a un emploi occasionnel________Elles ont des disputes occasionnel________

k. Le parc naturel__________attire beaucoup de touristes.

Unit 4. Other adjectives: for adjectives whose masculine ends in –ien – the feminine ends in -ienne

Masculine/sing	*Masc/pl.*	*Fem./sing*	*Fem/pl.*	*English*
-ien	*-iens*	*-ienne*	*-iennes*	
Ancien	anciens	ancienne	anciennes	former
Quotidien	quotidiens	quotidienne	quotidiennes	daily
Aérien	aériens	aérienne	aériennes	air, aerial
Aoûtien	aoûtiens	aoûtienne	aoûtiennes	August event

If the masculine of the Adjectives ends in –eux, the feminine ends in –euse. For such adjectives, the masculine singular and plural take the same form

Masc/sing	*Masc/pl*	*Fem/sing*	*Fem/pl*	*English meaning*
-eux	*-eux*	*-euse*	*-euses*	
Affreux	affreux	affreuse	affreuses	horrible
Capricieux	capricieux	capricieuse	capricieuses	capricious, whimsical
Heureux	heureux	heureuse	heureuses	happy
Sérieux	Sérieux	Sérieuse	Sérieuses	serious
Précieux	précieux	précieuse	précieuses	precious
Radieux	radieux	radieuse	radieuses	dazzling, radiant

If the masculine of the adjective ends in –if, the feminine will end in –ive

Masc/sing.	*Masc/pl*	*Fem/sing*	*Fem/pl*	*English*
-if	*-ifs*	*-ive*	*-ives*	
Actif	actifs	active	actives	active
Administratif	administratifs	administrative	administratives	administrative
Admiratif	admiratifs	admirative	admiratives	admiring
Attractif	attractifs	attractive	attractives	attractive
Compréhensif	compréhensifs	compréhensive	compréhensives	understanding
Impératif	impératifs	impérative	impératives	imperative/mandatory
Informatif	informatifs	informative	informatives	informative
Intensif	intensifs	intensive	intensives	intensive
Interactif	interactifs	interactive	interactives	interactive
Instructif	instructifs	instructive	instructives	instructive
Intuitif	intuitifs	intuitive	intuitives	intuitive

Invasif	invasifs	invasive	invasives	invasive
Maladif	maladifs	maladive	maladives	pathological, sickly
Massif	massifs	massive	massives	massive/mass
Figuratif	figuratifs	figurative	figuratives	figurative
Lucratif	lucratifs	lucrative	lucratives	gainful/profitable
Nominatif	nominatifs	nominative	nominatives	nominative
Normatif	normatifs	normative	normatives	prescriptive
Représentatif	représentatifs	représentative	représentatives	representative
Répressif	répressifs	répressive	répressives	repressive
Oppressif	oppressifs	oppressive	oppressives	oppressive
Passif	passifs	passive	passives	passive
Reproductif	reproductifs	reproductive	reproductives	reproductive
Répulsif	répulsifs	répulsive	répulsives	repulsive
Rétroactif	rétroactifs	rétroactive	rétroactives	retroactive
Rétrospectif	rétrospectifs	rétrospective	rétrospectives	retrospective
Répétitif	répétitifs	répétitive	répétitives	repetitive
Méditatif	méditatifs	méditative	méditatives	meditative/musing
Plaintif	plaintifs	plaintive	plaintives	plaintive/doleful
Craintif	craintifs	craintive	craintives	shy/timid
Rotatif	rotatifs	rotative	rotatives	rotary/rotating
Sportif	sportifs	sportive	sportives	sportsmanlike/fond of sports
Pulsatif	pulsatifs	pulsative	pulsatives	pulsative
Putatif	putatifs	putative	putatives	putative/presumed
Préventif	préventifs	préventive	préventives	preventive
Nocif	nocifs	nocive	nocives	harmful
Négatif	négatifs	négative	négatives	negative
Positif	positifs	positive	positives	positive
Primitif	primitifs	primitive	primitives	primitive/original
Fautif	fautifs	fautive	fautives	wrong, at fault

Adjectives in –al

Masc/sing. ***-al***	***Masc/plural*** ***-aux***	***Fem/sing*** ***-ale***	***Fem/plural*** ***-ales***	***English***
Amical	amicaux	amicale	amicales	friendly
Familial	familiaux	familiale	familiales	family
Fédéral	fédéraux	fédérale	fédérales	federal
Cantonal	cantonaux	cantonale	cantonales	cantonal

Royal	royaux	royale	royales	royal
Normal	normaux	normale	normales	normal
Animal	animaux	animale	animales animal/	raw/beastly
Fiscal	fiscaux	fiscale	fiscales	tax/fiscal
Pascal	pascaux	pascale	pascales	Easter
Médical	médicaux	médicale	médicales	medical
Municipal	municipaux	municipale	municipales	municipal
Principal	principaux	principale	principales	main/major
International	internationaux	internationale	internationales	international
National	nationaux	nationale	nationales	national
Régional	régionaux	régionale	régionales	regional
Trivial	triviaux	triviale	triviales	trivial
Electoral	électoraux	électorale	électorales	electoral
Egal	égaux	égale	égales	equal
Local	locaux	locale	locales	local
Mondial	mondiaux	mondiale	mondiales	world/world-wide
Communal	communaux	communale	communales	communal

Exercise 4.1 Choose the correct forms of adjectives, paying attention to the gender and number (singular and plural).

a. La route principal/principale est bloquée.

b. Les agents municipaux/municipales verbalisent les voitures mal garées.

c. Le témoin principal/principale est absent. Jacques a deux résidences principales/principaux.

d. Il y a 3 matches amicales/amicaux ce soir.

e. Il y a des litiges fiscales/fiscaux entre les deux pays.

f. Les magasins sont fermés pendant la fête pascal/pascale

g. Les élections municipales/municipaux ont lieu tous les deux ans.

h. Est-ce que ces frais médicales/médicaux sont couverts par l'assurance ?

i. Cette chanson a connu un succès mondial/mondiale.

j. Nous travaillons avec des partenaires locales/locaux

k. Leurs discussions portent sur des choses triviales/triviaux.

l. Les deux guerres mondiales/mondiaux ont fait beaucoup de victimes.

m. Les campagnes électorales/électorals sont lancées.

n. Les médecins sont tenus à garder les secrets médicaux/médicales de leurs patients.

Exercise 4.2. Choose the correct forms of adjectives

a. La révolution industrielle/industriel a eu des conséquences sur la vie social/sociale

b. La ville malienne/malien de Tombouctou a été inscrite au patrimoine mondiale/mondial de l'Unesco.

c. Deux buts ont été marqués pendant la première/premier mi-temps.

d. Le secteur financière/financier traverse une grave crise ces derniers/dernières temps.

e. Nous sommes inscrits auprès des agences immobilières/immobiliers.

f. Les clients fidèles/fidels reçoivent des rabais chaque année.

g. Deux employés sont jugés pour des transactions frauduleuses/frauduleux.

h. Les chiffres d'affaires trimestrielles/trimestriels ont doublé.

i. Le plan social/sociale prévoit des retraites anticipées/anticipés.

j. On demande une formation professionnelle/professionnel d'aide-soignante.

k. Les élections législatifs/législatives sont prévues en mars.

l. Une princesse amoureuse/amoureux est une princesse heureux/heureuse.

Exercise 4.3 Write the correct forms of the adjectives in relation to the nouns

a. Les services_______(social) de ce pays sont parmi les meilleurs au monde.

b. La_____________foire aux oignons a lieu chaque année. (traditionnel)

c. Les résultats sont_____________. (positif)

d. J'ai reçu un courrier______, une lettre _____________, si vous voulez (officiel)

e. C'est plutôt une histoire_____________(personnel)

f. Une maîtresse_______; un mari_____________(jaloux)

g. Des efforts ___________; la responsabilité _____________ (collectif)

h. Nous avons des temps_____; c'est une journée_____________(pluvieux)

i. L'_____________épouse; les_____________étudiants (ancien)

j. L'arrivée_____________ ; les dettes_____________(massif)

k. Un chanteur_____________ ; une actrice_____________(canadien)

l. Un échantillon_____________ ; des réponses_____________(représentatif)

m. Les soins_____________; les frappes_____________(intensif)

Unit 5. Adjectives in –os, -as

Masc/sing.	Masc/plural	Fem/sing	Fem/plural	English
-os/as	***-os/as***	***-osse/asse***	***-osses/-asses***	
Bas	bas	basse	basses	low
Gros	gros	grosse	grosses	fat/huge/big/thick
Gras	gras	grasse	grasses	fat/fatty/thick

E.g. ***Le bas revenu – low income ; les prix bas – low prices***

Un gros scandale, un gros homme d'affaires – a big scandal, a great businessman, un gros buveur – heavy drinker; un gros homme – a fat man
Une grosse femme – a fat woman ; une grosse voiture – a big car ; de grosses voitures – big cars

Adjectives in –on

Masc/sing.	Masc/pl.	Fem/sing	Fem/plural	English
-on	***-ons***	***-onne***	***-onnes***	
Bon	bons	bonne	bonnes	good
Mignon	mignons	mignonne	mignonnes	cute, sweet, nice, sweetheart
Con	cons	conne	connes	silly, stupid
Breton	bretons	bretonne	bretonnes	Breton
Marron	marrons	marronne	marronnes	quack/unqualified

Le monde breton; les villes bretonnes – the Brettany world; the Brettany cities
Un bon médecin – a good doctor; une bonne femme – a good woman; une bonne nouvelle – good news.

Adjectives ending in –eau

Masc/sing	***Masc/plural***	***Fem/sing***	***Fem/plural***	***English***
-eau	***-eaux***	***-elle***	***-elles***	
Beau	beaux	belle	belles	Beautiful, good-looking
Jumeau	jumeaux	jumelle	jumelles	twins
Nouveau	nouveaux	nouvelle	nouvelles	new
Vieux	vieux	vieille	vieilles	old

***Note that beau, nouveau, vieux become bel, nouvel, vieil before a masculine noun beginning with a vowel*:**

un bel homme, un nouvel étudiant, le vieil homme; le Nouvel An – the New Year; de beaux hommes – good-looking men, handsome men; de nouveaux étudiants – new students; les beaux-arts – fine arts

This rule does not apply to female nouns beginning with a vowel: Nouvelle Ecosse – Nova Scotia; Nouvelle Angleterre – New England; une nouvelle étudiante – a new student

Frais	frais	fraiche	fraiches	cool/chilly, fresh
Doux	doux	douce	douces	smooth, soft, sweet
public	publics	publique	publiques	public
Mou	Mous	molle	molles	soft, slack, weak
Fou	fous	folle	folles	mad/crazy
Blanc	blancs	blanche	blanches	white
Franc	francs	franche	franches	frank, straightforward, candid
Long	longs	longue	longues	long
Bénin	bénins	bénigne	bénignes	mild, harmless, benign, minor
Malin	malins	maligne	malignes	cunning, crafty, malignant
Sec	secs	sèche	sèches	dry

Unit 6. Indefinite adjectives – plusieurs, quelques, certains, certaines, un/une autre, l'autre, d'autres, les autres, chaque, le, la même ; les mêmes ; tout, toute, tous les ; toutes les; aucun(e) - non

Indefinite adjectives are those adjectives that are not precise about the nouns they relate to. Whether they describe ***quantity*** – several, many, some, a few; ***similarity*** – the same; ***difference*** – another, the other, others; or the ***whole*** – all, every; there is no clarity or precision in terms of the meaning. They are vague and leave a wide range of interpretations.

Quantity: ***plusieurs*** personnes, ***plusieurs*** passagers, ***plusieurs*** élèves, ***plusieurs*** enfants, ***plusieurs*** hommes et femmes – many/several people, pupils, children, men and women.
Plusieurs is plural and is the same for both genders. ***Many/several*** means different things to different people.

Aucun(e) - none
Aucun étudiant n'est en retard aujourd'hui – no student is late today
Aucune monitrice ne travaille la nuit – no instructor/coach works at night

Un autre rendez–vous – another appointment
Une autre voiture – another car
L'autre rendez-vous – the other appointment
L'autre voiture – the other car
Les autres garçons – the other boys, les autres filles – the other girls
D'autres systèmes, d'autres coutumes – other systems, other customs

Quelques manifestants réclament la démission du président – some/a few demonstrators want the president to step down.

Certains étudiants ne font pas leurs devoirs (m/pl – some students don't do their homework.
Certaines patientes sont végétariennes (fem/pl) – some patients are vegetarian.

Similarity: ***le/la même, les mêmes*** – the same
C'est le même résultat – It is the same result
C'est la même chose – it is the same thing
J'ai les mêmes livres – I have the same books;
Elle voit les mêmes voitures, les mêmes personnes. – She sees the same cars, the same persons.

The whole: ***tout le*** bureau – the entire office (masc/sing);
Tous les bureaux – all the offices (masc/plural)
Toute la classe (fem/sing) – the whole class/the entire class;
Toutes les classes (fem/plural) – all the classes

Note that tout le + plural = tous les : tous les jours, tous les garçons, tous les hommes, tous les chemins.
Toute + les (plural = toutes les) : toutes les semaines, toutes les classes, toutes les filles, toutes les femmes, toutes les règles.

Exercise 6.1 ***Complete the sentences with the correct forms of the adjectives***

E.g. Il travaille___________les jours (tout). – Il travaille *tous* les jours

a. ___________nos lignes sont occupées (tout)

b. ___________incident majeur n'est à signaler (aucun/aucune)

c. ___________données sont volées (Certains/Certaines)

d. Les résultats sont___________(le/la/ les même/mêmes)

e. ___________l'aiment chaud.___________l'aiment froid (Certain/certains. les autres/d'autres.)

f. Voici___________conseils pour expliquer le jeu (plusieurs/quelques).

g. ___________nos plats sont chauds (toutes/tous)

h. ___________place n'est réservée (aucun/aucune)

i. Il pleut___________la journée (tout/toute)

j. Il n'y a aucun/aucune rabais cette semaine.

Exercise 6.2 ***Continue the same exercise.***

a. ___________pièce est unique. (chaque/chacune).

b. ___________changement d'adresse doit être signalé. (toute/tout)

c. ___________voisins sont sympathiques (certains/certaines).___________sont indifférents. (Les autres/D'autres)

d. Nous aimons___________les styles de musique.(toutes/tous)

e. ___________les routes mènent à Rome. (toutes/tous)

f. Le tremblement de terre n'a duré que quelques/quelque secondes.

g. La chaine NTA cite plusieurs/plusieures sources bien informées.

h. Selon les prévisions de la météo, il va pleuvoir tout/toute la journée demain.

Unit 7. Indefinite pronouns

1. ***Quelqu'un*** veut voir Monsieur Ade. – Someone wants to see Mr Ade
2. ***Certains*** aiment le riz au poulet. – Some like chicken rice
3. ***D'autres*** adorent l'igname aux sauces piquantes. – Others love yam with hot sauce.
4. ***Personne*** ne répond à ce genre d'annonce – Nobody replies this kind of advertisement
5. ***Aucune*** des parties n'accepte la proposition de l'autre – None of the parties accepts the other's proposition.
6. ***Rien*** n'a changé depuis ton départ. – Nothing has changed since you left.

Indefinite pronouns are used to refer to someone or something that is not clear or specified. In the first example above, we are told that ***someone*** (***quelqu'un***) ***wants to see Mr Ade***, but we have no idea who that can be.

The second example informs us that ***some like chicken rice***, but gives no indication as to who ***certains*** (some) refers to.

In the same manner, example 3 indicates ***others***, example 4 ***nobody***, while 5 and 6 mention ***none*** and ***nothing*** respectively.

Quelqu'un (someone), quelque chose (something), certains/certaines (some), un/une autre, (another), l'autre (the other), les autres (the others)
d'autres (others)

Exercise 7.1 ***Replace the underlined words with indefinite pronouns, as in the example.***

Bonjour à tous les participants et à toutes les participantes – Bonjour à tous et à toutes.

a. Elle contrôle toutes les données.

b. Chaque participant doit s'inscrire sur notre site.

c. Chaque pièce coûte N30'000.

d. Plusieurs patients considèrent la médecine traditionnelle nécessaire.

e. Notre porte est ouverte à tous mes amis.

f. Nous luttons pour que tous les enfants aient accès à la scolarité.

g. Quelques personnes arrivent maintenant.

h. Certaines informations ne sont pas vérifiables.

Negation pronouns: note the double negation

Personne – nobody; ***aucun/aucune*** – none; ***rien*** – nothing

Personne ne répond – Nobody is answering/responding.
Il n'y a personne à la maison. – There is nobody at home.
Personne ne m'a cru. – Nobody believed me.

Elle ***ne*** dit ***rien*** – she is not saying anything;
Robert a tout perdu. – Robert lost everything. Il ***n***'a plus ***rien***. – He doesn't have anything anymore.

Rien - nothing: ***Rien*** ne marche pour l'instant. – Nothing is working at the moment.
Je n'ai ***rien*** mangé. I ate nothing; Elle n'a ***rien*** vu. – She saw nothing.
Est-ce que Pascal a donné quelquechose? Did Pascal give anything ?
Non, il n'a ***rien*** donné. No, he gave nothing (he didn't give anything)

Aucun/aucune –none:
Est-ce qu'on a des preuves? – Non, ***aucune***! Nous n'avons ***aucune***.
Do we have evidence? – No, none. We have none**.**

Aucun de nous ne joue au football. – None of us plays football**.**
Laquelle de ces chansons t'a plu? – ***Aucune*** ! Which of these songs did you like? – None!
Lequel de ces hôtels est bon marché? – ***Aucun***! Which of these hotels is cheap? – None!
Aucun ne me plait. – I don't like any.

Est-ce que les amies de Catherine sont venues? Did Catherine's friends come?
Non, ***aucune n'est*** venue. – No, none came.

Note: Aucun ne...; personne ne...; rien ne ...: These expresssions are accompanied by negations:
Aucun n'est venu – none came/has come.
Je ne vois aucun – I don't see any

Personne n'a téléphoné. - Nobody has called.
Il n'y a personne – There is nobody.

Rien ne marche – Nothing is working.

Exercise 7.2 Answer the questions in the negative

E.g. Est-ce que vous voulez manger quelque chose? – Non, je ne veux rien manger.

a. Est-ce que tu vois quelqu'un? – Je ne vois personne________(personne)

b. Est-ce que tous ses rêves se réalisent? – Non,_______________(aucun)

c. Est-ce que tout va bien? – Non,________________________(rien)

d. Est-ce que mes invités sont là? – Non,________________(aucun).

e. Est-ce que Madame attend quelqu'un? – Non, elle________(personne)

f. Est-ce que les enfants veulent boire quelque chose? – Non, ils________(rien)

g. Est-ce que l'appareil répond à toutes vos attentes? – Non, il________à (aucune)

h. Est-ce que tout le monde est satisfait? – Non,________________(personne)

i. Est-ce que vous comprenez tout en Français? – Non,________(rien) en français

j. Avez-vous quelque chose à déclarer? – Non,________________à déclarer (rien).

Exercise 7.3 Supply the missing indefinite pronouns

E.g. J'ai très faim. Je veux manger (quelque chose)

(Use these pronouns: tout, tous, quelqu'un, certains, d'autres, quelques-unes, chacun, chacune)

a. Sandra a envie de parler avec____

b. Venez, car________est prêt

c. __________pensent que le médecin est coupable.__________pensent qu'il est innocent.

d. Toutes les voitures ne sont pas rentrées aux garages. Il manque________________

e. ________veut parler au président.

f. Ici, c'est________pour soi, Dieu pour__________

g. ________des joueuses veut gagner le tournoi.

Unit 8. French verbs: the –er verbs with constant radicals: Present tense

Category 1A verbs

Common-endings conjugation.

The verbs in this group end in "***er***" and have ***constant radicals***. To obtain the radical from each verb, drop the "***er***" from the infinitive. We create a conjugation formula which is applicable to all verbs in the group.

To conjugate any verb in this group, add the radical to the endings corresponding to the personal pronouns.

The ***personal pronouns are: Je/j', tu, il/elle, nous, vous, ils/elles***

Use ***j'*** if the verbs begin with a vowel: ***j'abaisse, j'écoute, j'accepte***

These are the radicals of the verbs: ***abaiss-, abdiqu-, accept-, biff-, baign, écout***;

These are the 6 conjugation endings for categories 1 -8 verbes: ***e es e ons ez ent***

Je	e
Tu demand-	es
Il/elle	e
Nous	ons
Vous	ez
Ils/elles	ent

		Je/j'	***tu***	***il/elle***	***nous***	***vous***	***ils/elles***
		e	***es***	***e***	***ons***	***ez***	***ent***
abaisser	abaiss-						
accepter	accept-						
blesser	bless-						
créer	cré-						
danser	dans-						

J'abaiss***e***	tu abaiss***es***	il/elle abaiss***e***	nous abaiss***ons***	vous abaiss***ez***	ils/elles abaiss***ent***
J'accept***e***	tu accept***es***	il/elle accept***e***	nous accept***ons***	vous accept***ez***	ils/elles accept***ent***
Je bless***e***	tu bless***es***	il/elle blesse	nous bless***ons***	vous bless***ez***	ils/elles bless***ent***
je cré***e***	tu cré***es***	il/elle cré***e***	nous cré***ons***	vous cré***ez***	ils/elles cré***ent***
je dans***e***	tu dans***es***	il/elle dans***e***	nous dans***ons***	vous dans***ez***	ils/elles dans***ent***

Je/j'	***tu***	***il/elle***	***nous***	***vous***	***ils/elles***
e	***es***	***e***	***ons***	***ez***	***ent***

abîmer	abîm-
aborder	abord-
baigner	baign-
baliser	balis-
bloquer	bloqu-
biffer	biff-
câbler	câbl-
cacher	cach-
calculer	calcul-
calibrer	calibr-
casser	cass-
causer	caus-
cultiver	cultiv-

Choose any verb in the group/category, and combine the radical with endings.

Conjugation Formula = tense radicals + tense endings

For a verb such as ***parler***, present ***tense format*** is: ***parl- + e + es + e + ons + ez + ent***

Je parl***e*** tu parl***es*** il/elle parl***e*** nous parl***ons*** vous parl***ez*** ils/elles parl***ent***

Associate the pronouns with their endings :
j'accept***e*** tu accept***es*** il/elle accept***e*** nous accept***ons*** vous accept***ez*** ils/elles accept***ent***

Elles acceptent le travail comme un nouveau défi. They accept the job as a new challenge.

Note: Use ***j'*** if the verb begins with a vowel:

J'aim***e*** les langues – I love languages; j'aim***e*** voyager – I love travelling

J'écout***e*** la radio – I am listening to the radio

J'ador***e*** l'acteur, la chanteuse – I adore the actor, the singer.
Tu ador***es*** la comedienne; you love the actress ; tu regard***es*** la télé. – you watch TV.
Tu écout***es*** les informations – you listen to the news.

Je ferm***e*** la boutique à 18h. – I close the shop at 6 p.m.

Tu ferm***es*** toujours ta voiture à clé. – You always lock your car

Nous ferm***ons*** le bureau à 17h00. We close the office at 5 p.m.

Vous parl***ez*** yoruba. You speak Yoruba. Vous aim***ez*** la musique.

Elles ferm***ent*** la porte avant de sortir – They close the door before going out.

Ada et sa soeur ont une belle voix. Elles chant***ent*** bien.
Ada and her sister have a beautiful voice. They sing well.

Les enfants jou***ent*** au parc. The children are playing in the park

Mes amis regard***ent*** les chaines sportives. – My friends watch sports channels.

Memorize the ending corresponding to each personal pronoun.

Exercise 8.1 Conjugate the verbs in present tense.

a. J'________souvent ce que je________.(oublier/chercher)

b. A quelle heure est-ce que vous______________à Lagos ? (arriver)

c. Tu______________inviter combien de personnes à ton anniversaire? (compter)

d. J'_____10 personnes, mais ce sont 50 personnes qui__________-(inviter/arriver)

e. Quand vous_______les élèves, ils__________mieux. (encourager/travailler)

f. Elles_______avec le patron qui_______certaines propositions. (négocier/accepter)

g. Je_____mes vacances à Obudu. Où est-ce que tu________tes vacances ? (passer)

h. Chaque année, nous____________nos copains pendant les vacances. (retrouver)

i. Il te____________de laisser ton numéro de téléphone. (demander)

Exercise 8.2. Put into negative

E.g. J'écoute la radio tous les jours – Je n'écoute pas la radio tous les jours
I listen to the radio everyday - I don't listen to the radio everyday

Nous montrons nos émotions – Nous ne montrons pas nos émotions.
We show our feelings – We don't show our feelings

Elle explique la situation – Elle n'explique pas la situation
She explains the situation – she does not explain the situation

a. Nous gagnons bien notre vie. -________________________________

b. Vous habitez à Ikeja________________________________

c. J'habite en Suisse________________________________

d. Qui *cherche trouve*________________________________(2 verbs to be put into negative)

e. Ils indiquent leur nouvelle adresse.________________________________

f. Tu trouves ces photos belles________________________________

g. Vous respectez la loi.________________________________

h. Ils aident les personnes en difficulté.________________________________

i. Il danse comme Michael Jackson.________________________________

j. Elles écoutent tes conseils.________________________________

k. La ville attire les jeunes.________________________________

l. L'arbitre regarde sa montre.________________________________

m. Ces footballeurs jouent à Madrid.________________________________

n. Je téléphone à mes parents tous les jours.________________________________

o. Ada justifie la confiance qu'on lui fait.________________________________

Unit 9. The imperative mood.

Use the imperative to urge people to do something, to give instructions or advice, or to dissuade them from doing something.

Tu dois parler avec Susan. – Parle avec Susan. You should speak with Susan. Speak with Susan.
Vous devez parler de la situation au chef. – Parlez de la situation au chef.

You should speak to the boss about the situation. – Speak about the situation to the boss.
Nous devons parler du match de ce soir. – Parlons du match de ce soir.
We should talk about this evening's match. Let's talk about this evening's match.

Tu dois préchauffer le four pendant 10 minutes. – Préchauffe le four pendant 10 minutes.
You have to preheat the oven for 10 minutes. Preheat the oven for 10 minutes.

Versez le contenu de la boîte dans l'eau bouillante. Pour the content of the can into boiling. water
Jouons à cache-cache. – Let's play hide and seek.

Chantons les chants de Noël ! Let's sing Christmas songs.

Exercise 9.1 Put these sentences into the imperative form

Example: Vous devez *aimer* votre pays. You should love your country. – Aimez votre pays. – Love your country

Tu dois aimer ton prochain. – *Aime* ton prochain. Love your neighbour

Nous devons *jouer* ensemble. – Jouons ensemble. – Let's play together

a. Tu dois *regarder* le programme ce soir. -______________________________

b. Vous devez *expliquer* le problème à John. -______________________________

c. Nous devons *aider* le père Noël. -______________________________

d. Vous devez *surfer* sur internet. -______________________________

e. Tu dois *parler* maintenant. -______________________________

f. Vous devez *présenter* vos papiers, s'il vous plaît. -______________________________

g. Nous devons *demander* à Pascal. -______________________________

h. Monsieur l'arbitre, vous devez *siffler* la fin du match. -______________________________

i. Tu dois *rester* calme, bébé. -______________________________

j. Nous devons *fêter* cette belle victoire. -______________________________

Unit 10. The imperative in the negative

Use the negative imperative to urge someone not to do something

Ne traversez pas la rue quand le feu est au rouge. Don't cross the road when the light is red.
Ne quitte pas le pays maintenant. – Don't leave the country now.

Tournez à gauche, à droite. Turn left, right.

– Ne tournez pas à gauche, ou à droite. - Don't turn left or right.

Ne conservez pas la nourriture au-délà de la date indiquée – don't keep food beyond the date indicated.

N'oublions pas d'éteindre les lumières en sortant. – Let's not forget to put the lights off when going out.

Ne publiez pas votre vie privée sur le réseau social. – Don't publish your private life on the social network.

Ne verse pas l'argent sur son compte. – Don't pay the money into his account.

Exercise 10.1 Translate the sentences into French, using the expressions supplied.

E.g. Don't start again – (recommencer); (signer le contrat); frapper à la porte) Ne recommence pas; Don't sign the contract – Ne signez pas le contrat ; let's not knock – ne frappons pas à la porte

a. Don't burn the bridges. – Ne brûlez pas les ponts. (brûler les ponts)

b. Don't give him your number. -____________________.(lui donner ton numéro)

c. Don't forget to take your medicine____________________.(Oublier_____de prendre votre médicament)

d. Don't listen to him; don't listen to them.__________________;__________________.(écouter)

e. Don't increase taxes. -___________________________(augmenter les impôts)

f. Don't insult your friends. -____________________(insulter tes amis)

g. Don't ring.____________________Le bébé dort. (sonner).

h. Don't sign a contract if you don't understand it. ______________________________
(Signer un contrat si vous ne le comprenez pas).

i. Don't forget to lock the door. -____________________(oublier de fermer la porte à clé.)

j. Let's not talk about the problem. (Parler du problème)

k. Let's not park on the pavement (garer la voiture sur le trottoir)

l. Don't disturb me.____(déranger)

Unit 11. The imperative and the positions of object pronouns.

The imperative in the affirmative mood.

Passe-***moi*** le dictionnaire, s'il te plaît – Give me the dictionary, please

Donnez-***moi*** le stylo, s'il vous plaît - Give ***me*** the pen, please

Prêtez-***nous*** $10'000, s'il vous plaît – Lend us $10'000, please.

Prête-***lui*** ton jouet. – Lend him your toy.

Montre-***moi*** la photo - show me the photo; montrez-***nous*** la photo –show us the photo.

In the affirmative, the objects – whether direct or indirect – are placed directly after the verb.

In the ***negative***, the object come before the verb; ***moi*** becomes ***me,*** while ***toi*** becomes ***te***

Dépêche-***toi*** – hurry up. Ne ***te*** dépêche pas – don't hurry up
Cache-***toi*** – hide ; ne ***te*** cache pas – don't hide

1. Passe-***moi*** le dictionnaire - Ne ***me passe*** pas le dictionnaire – don't give me the dictionary
2. Ne lui ***donnez*** pas le stylo - don't give her/him the pen
3. Ne leur ***prêtez*** pas $10'000. – don't lend them $10'000.
4. Ne lui ***prête*** pas ton jouet - don't lend him/her your toy.
5. Ne me ***montrez*** pas la photo ; ne nous montrez pas la photo. – don't show us the photo.
6. Ne le dérangez pas. – Don't disturb him.
7. Ne jouez pas avec moi. – Don't play with me.

In sentences 1-5, me, nous, lui are indirect object because action of the verb passes to the pronouns through a preposition ***to,*** though we can't see it.

Ne m'aide pas – don't help me. N'aidons pas le père Noël. –Let us not help Father Christmas.

Conseillez-moi sur ce qu'il faut faire. – Advise me on what to do
Ne me conseillez pas sur ce qu'il faut faire. – Don't advise me on what to do.

Exercise 11.1 Change the sentences into negative, according to the example.

E.g. Montre-moi ton cadeau. – Ne me montre pas ton cadeau. Appelez-les. - Ne les appelez pas

a. Expliquez-nous le problème. -________________________________

b. Attrape-le, s'il te plaît. -________________________________

c. Regardez-moi dans les yeux. -________________________________

d. Écoutons-le.________________________________

e. Écoute-les.________________________________

f. Montre-lui le chemin. -________________________________

g. Donne-moi son numéro de téléphone. -________________________________

h. Cachez-la chez-vous. -________________________________

i. Contacte-moi ; contactez-nous ; contactons-les; Téléphone-lui tout de suite________________

____

Exercise 12.2.Continue the same exercise on imperative negative

Laissez-les entrer. – Let them come in. – Ne les laissez pas entrer. Don't let them come in.

a. Racontez votre vie privée sur Facebook. ________________________________

b. Commente cette affaire à la radio ou à la télé. ________________________________

c. Écoute ce qu'ils disent. ________________________________

d. Donnez-lui une deuxième chance.________________________________

e. Lave ton linge sale en public. ________________________________

f. Prêtez votre dictionnaire à Oge. ________________________________

g. Parlons de l'incident. ________________________________

h. Contactez-moi après 21 heures. ________________________________

i. Regarde trop la télévision. ________________________________

Unit 12. Interrogative mood

Use the interrogative forms below to ask questions:

(1) ***Est-ce que/qu'...?***

(2) ***By inverting the positions of the subject and the verb***

(3) ***By intonation***

(1) ***Est-ce que/qu'....?***

Vous parlez français. Tu parles français. You speak French.

Vous parlez français. - ***Est-ce que*** vous parlez français? ***Est-ce que*** tu parles français ? – Do you speak French ?

Il écoute tes conseils. ***Est-ce qu'***il écoute tes conseils ? Does he listen to your advice?

Elle danse bien. - ***Est-ce qu'***elle danse bien ? – Does she dance well ?

Ils habitent à Owerri. - Est-ce qu'ils habitent à Owerri ? Do they live in Owerri?

2) B***y inverting the positions of the subject and the verb***

Vous parlez français. ***Parlez-vous*** français?

Tu parles allemand. Parles-tu allemand? – Do you speak German?

Il parle igbo. Parle-t-il iIgbo? – Does he speak Igbo?

Vous aimez les animaux. Aimez-vous les animaux? – Do you love animals?

Tu aimes le football. Aimes-tu le football? – Do you like football?

Elle aime ce travail. - Aime-***t***-elle ce travail? - Does she like this job?

Elles aiment les cadeaux. Aiment-elles les cadeaux? – Do they like the presents?

Use ***-t-*** as a linking consonant when the verb ends in a vowel and the pronoun begins also with a vowel:

Elle regarde la télévision. Regard***e***-t-elle la télévision? Does she watch television ?

Il aime l'école. Aim***e***-t-il l'école? – Does he like school?

By intonation

Vous aimez votre pays can be an affirmation or a question depending on the intonation.

Compare: Il aime l'école. – He likes school. Il aime l'école? – Does he like school?

Ils parlent bien français. – They speak good French.

Ils parlent bien français? – Do they speak good French?

Exercise 12.1 Put these sentences into the interrogative form according to the examples

Vous parlez chinois. – Parlez-vous chinois?

Elle maîtrise l'arabe. – Maîtrise-t-elle l'arabe?

Tu entres sans frapper. – Entres-tu sans frapper ?

Ils dansent très bien. - Dansent-ils très bien ?

a. Toyota fabrique de belles voitures.____________________

b. Vous maîtrisez les outils informatiques. -____________________

c. Il allume toujours la télé quand il se réveille. -____________________

d. Ce papier atteste que Kemi est malade. -____________________

e. Vous signez tout de suite un contrat de travail chez-nous. -____________________

f. Elle explique pourquoi elle divorce. -____________________

g. Il souhaite ouvrir un compte dans une banque. -____________________

h. Tu casses la voiture au lieu de la réparer. -____________________

i. Vous travaillez à 100%. -____________________

j. Ils portent les mêmes costumes qu'hier. -____________________

k. Vous admirez les fleurs.____________________

l. Vous avez des animaux domestiques.____________________

Unit 13. Pronominal or reflexive verbs: present tense

Pronominal verbs, also called reflexive verbs, are those verbs having the subject as also the object of the action. The subject feels his action, and thus becomes also the object of the verb.

E.g. ***I wash myself,*** (as opposed to I wash the baby, the dish); ***we wake up – we wake ourselves up***, not woken by someone); ***she brushes her teeth – her own teeth, not her son's or her daughter's***, etc. The author of the action is also the receiver.

	Je me/m'	***tu te/t'***	***il/elle se/s'***	***nous nous***	***vous vous***	***ils/elles se/s'***
Tense formula: radical + :	***e***	***es***	***e***	***ons***	***ez***	***ent***

S'amuser	1.	je m' amus-	e	(1)
Se dépêcher	2.	tu t'	es	(2)
Se demander	3.	il/elle s'	e	(3)
Se laver	4.	nous nous	ons	(4)
S'informer	5.	vous vous inform-	ez	(5)
Se fâcher	6.	ils/elles s' intéress-	ent	(6)
S'intéresser				

Je me	demand-	e
Tu te		es
Il/elle se	couch-	e
Nous nous		ons
Vous vous		ez
Ils/elles se		ent

Se déguiser	déguis-
Se blesser	bless-
Se coucher	couch-
Se doucher	douch-

Je m'amus***e*** tu t'amus***es*** il s'amus***e*** nous nous amus***ons*** vous vous amus***ez*** ils s'amus***ent***

Je me douch***e*** tu te douch***es*** il se douch***e*** nous nous douch***ons*** v.v douch***ez*** ils se douch***ent***

(Se doucher – to shower : ***Je me*** douch***e*** à 6h00 du matin. I shower at 6 a.m.
Nous nous douch***ons***, ***vous vous*** douch***ez***, ***ils se*** douch***ent***).

Note the double personal pronouns in each sentence. The first is the subject, while the second is the direct object. This means that the author of the action is also the receiver of the action.

Use ***je m', tu t', il s', elle s', ils s', elles s'***, if the verb begins with a ***vowel*** or a ***h***
Je m'amus***e***, tu t'amus***es***, elle s'amus***e***, nous nous amus***ons***, vous vous amus***ez***, elles s'amus***ent***
Note: use se/s' for 3rd person singular or plural:

Il se douche - He is having a shower; elle s'amuse – she is playing, having fun (singular)
Papa ***se*** ras***e*** tous les matins (singular) – Papa shaves every morning

Ils ***se*** rasent; elles s'amusent; ils se cachent; elles se coiffent - plural

D'habitude, les femmes ***se*** maquill***ent*** avant de sortir. Women usually put on make-up before going out.

Note: Je ***m'***intéresse tu ***t'***intéresses il/elle ***s'***intéresse ils/elles ***s'***intéressent
Je ***m'***amuse tu ***t'***amuses il/elle ***s'***amuse ils/elles ***s'***amusent

No ellipsis for « ***nous*** » and « ***vous*** »: ***nous nous amusons, vous vous amusez***

Exercise 13.1

Conjugate these pronominal verbs, using the persons indicated; the above examples can help you:

a. Elle__________les doigts chaque fois qu'elle fait la cuisine (se brûler)

b. Les enfants__________bien au parc (s'amuser)

c. Mais là tu__________sur tes lauriers (se reposer)

d. Plusieurs couples__________(se marier) à des dates fétiches telles que 01.01.2001; 06.06. 2006; 09.09. 2009; 10.10. 2010; 11.11. 2011; 12.12. 2012

e. En ce moment, je__________à Lagos (se trouver)

f. Où, à Lagos, est-ce que vous__________? (se trouver)

g. Le magicien______________en une vieille femme. (se transformer).

h. Nous_______________dans le miroir avant de sortir (se regarder)

i. Les candidats______________beaucoup de questions (se poser)

j. Aujourd'hui, je_______________tu______________,nous __________ ______________ facilement sur internet (se connecter)

Unit 13B. Pronominal verbs in the interrogative mood

With pronominal verbs, sentences can be constructed in the interrogative mood in three ways:

1. By placing the interrogative clause "***est-ce que***" at the beginning of the sentence.

   Vous vous couchez avant minuit. – ***Est-ce que*** vous vous couchez avant minuit ?

   Vous vous occupez bien de vos enfants. – ***Est-ce que*** vous vous occupez bien de vos enfants ?

   Elle se couche tard. – ***Est-ce qu'***elle se couche tard ?

   Ils se reposent sur leurs lauriers. – ***Est-ce qu'***ils se reposent sur leurs lauriers ?

   Tu t'amuses bien. – ***Est-ce que*** tu t'amuses bien ?

   Nous nous marions en décembre. – ***Est-ce que*** nous nous marions en décembre?

2. **By inverting the sentence in such a way that the object will be at the beginning, followed by the verb and then the subject:**

Je me trouve à Genève –	me trouve-je à Genève?
Tu te déguises en sorcier –	Te déguises-tu en sorcier ?
Tu t'amuses bien avec tes copains.	T'amuses-tu bien avec tes copains ?
Il se trompe encore –	se trompe-t-il encore ?
Il s'occupe bien de ses enfants.	S'occupe-t-il bien de ses enfants ?
Elle se couche tard –	Se couche-t-elle tard ?
Elle s'intéresse beaucoup au tennis.	S'intéresse-t-elle beaucoup au tennis ?
Nous nous réveillons tous après un mauvais rêve.	Nous réveillons-nous tous après un mauvais rêve ?
Nous nous amusons bien à la fête.	Nous amusons-nous bien à la fête ?
Vous vous trouvez à Londres.	Vous trouvez-vous à Londres ?
Ils s'habillent très chaud en hiver.	S'habillent-ils très chaud en hiver ?
Ils se trompent de numéro.	Se trompent-ils de numéro ?

Elles s'adressent à la police.	S'adressent-elles à la police ?
Elles se méfient de certains clients.	Se méfient-elles de certains clients ?

3. ***By intonation. You can use the intonation to indicate the interrogative mood.***

Elle s'adresse à la police.	Elle s'adresse à la police ?
Vous vous trouvez à Paris	Vous vous trouvez à Paris ?

Exercise 13B.1 Put the following sentences in the interrogative, using:

(1) ***est-ce que/qu'*** (2) ***by inverting their order***

a. Elles s'informent de leur père qui est malade.____________________

b. Tu te fies toujours aux apparences.____________________

c. Ils se déshabillent devant tout le monde.____________________

d. Vous vous posez toujours cette question.____________________

e. La sorcière se transforme en une jeune femme très belle.____________________

f. Ils s'adressent au chef.____________________

g. Elle se marie sans l'accord de ses parents.____________________

h. Il se regarde dans le miroir.____________________

i. Vous vous adaptez à ces nouvelles situations.____________________

j. Nous nous cachons la caverne.____________________

k. Ils s'imaginent supérieurs à tout le monde.____________________

l. Tu t'occupes des enfants de ta sœur.____________________

m. Elles s'intéressent aux mathématiques.____________________

n. Vous vous préparez pour les examens.____________________

Unit 14. Pronominal verbs in the imperative mood.

As we saw earlier, we use the imperative form to urge, give instructions, order, advice or persuade people to do something.

Tu te regardes dans le miroir - Regarde-toi dans le miroir – look at yourself in the mirror.

Vous vous regardez. Regardez-vous! (Look at yourself/yourselves 2nd person singular/plural).

Use ***vous*** as singular in formal situations, and as plural in both formal and informal situations.

Nous nous cachons - Cachons-nous vite – Let's hide quickly.

Cache-toi vite (2nd person singular : informal) – hide yourself quickly

Cachez-vous derrière l'armoire – hide yourselves behind the wardrobe (2nd person /plural)

Cachons-nous sous le lit ! - Let's hide under the bed.

Amuse-toi bien – Amusez-vous bien – Have fun, enjoy yourself/yourselves

Amusons-nous (1st person plural) – let's play, let's have fun

Note that for ***–er verbs***, we drop ***s*** in ***the <u>imperative</u>*** for ***2nd person singular: regarde-toi, amuse-toi; renseigne-toi; cache-toi.***

Exercise 14. Put these verbs in the imperative form.

E.g. S'amuser: Amuse-toi; amusez-vous; amusons-nous!

a. _________-nous d'acheter des billets. Le match va commencer. (se dépêcher)
_________-toi, Ada. Et vous, les enfants,_____________-vous. (se dépêcher)

b. _________-vous en avant pour admirer le paysage. (se pencher)

c. _________-toi bien à la barre, sinon tu vas tomber. (s'accrocher)

d. _________-nous à l'ombre. Il fait très chaud. (s'installer)

e. _________-vous des inconnus sur le web. (se méfier)

f. N'aie pas peur ! _________-toi du chien. Il est gentil. (s'approcher)

g. _________-vous, Monsieur! Nous avons un problème technique. (se calmer)

h. _________-toi par terre. L'herbe est propre (se coucher)

i. _________-nous maintenant, car on va partir très tôt demain matin. (se coucher)

j. _________-vous bien. Vous allez aff ronter une grande équipe. (se préparer)

k. _________-nous. Il y a de l'eau chaude. (se baigner)

l. _________-toi. Tout va bien. (se calmer)

Unit 14B. Pronominal Verbs: the negative imperative mood

We use the negative imperative to give instructions or advice on what should not be done.

Imperatives in the affirmative	***the negative imperative***
Approche-toi- Come closer	Ne t'approche pas – don't come closer
Approchez-vous!	Ne vous approchez pas
Approchons-nous – let us come closer	Ne nous approchons pas – let's not get close
Dépêche-toi- hurry up	Ne te dépêche pas – don't hurry.
Dépêchez-vous	Ne vous dépêchez pas
Dépêchons-nous – let's hurry up	Ne nous dépêchons pas – Let's not hurry

Note that while in the affirmative, the <u>pronoun comes after the verb</u>, in the negative imperative, the pronoun precedes the verb.

Note also that <u>toi</u> in the affirmative becomes <u>te</u> in the negative.

Exercise 14B.1. Rewrite these sentences after the models

Repose-toi maintenant – Ne te repose pas maintenant.

Penchez-vous sur la fenêtre – Ne vous penchez pas sur la fenêtre

Fions-nous aux apparences – Ne nous fions pas aux apparences

a. Cache-toi.______________________________

b. Amusez-vous avec un revolver.______________________________

c. Approche-toi d'un lion qui dort. -______________________________

d. Dépêchons-nous. Le match va commencer. -______________________________

e. Cachez-vous derrière la porte. -______________________________

f. Douche-toi avec l'eau froide. -______________________________

g. Occupez-vous de ses problèmes. -______________________________

h. Éloignons-nous du sujet. -______________________________

i. Occupe-toi des choses terrestres. -____

Forming the negative of pronominal verbs

To form the negative of the pronominal verb, place the pronominal verb between the negative particles ne......pas.

The verb is usually preceded by the second pronoun which is the object.

Je me réveille à 5 heures. - Je ne me réveille pas à 5 heures.
Tu t'habilles chaud. Tu ne t'habilles pas chaud

Elle s'adapte à sa nouvelle situation. – Elle ne s'adapte pas à sa nouvelle situation.
Je m'adresse à la police. - Je ne m'adresse pas à la police

Tu t'occupes de mes affaires. - Tu ne t'occupes pas de mes affaires.
Il se mêle aux affaires des autres. - Il ne se mêle pas aux affaires des autres

Nous nous amusons dans le froid. - Nous ne nous amusons pas dans le froid.
Vous vous fiez facilement aux apparances. - Vous ne vous fiez pas facilement aux apparences.
you don't easily let appearances deceive you.

Ils s'éloignent du but. - Ils ne s'éloignent pas du but – they don't wander off the target/goal

Subject + ne + pronominal vb + pas.

Paul se rase tous les jours. Paul ne ***se rase*** pas tous les jours.

Se méfier de quelqu'un or de quelque chose – To distrust someone or something, be suspicious of; beware of,

Je me méfie de cet homme. – I don't trust this man

Je ne ***me méfie*** pas de cet homme - I am not suspicious of this man

Tu te méfies de ces produits - You should be careful about these products

Tu ne ***te méfies*** pas de ces produits You trust these products

Se brosser les dents – to brush one's teeth – je me brosse les dents le matin et le soir

S'occuper de quelqu'un/quelque chose – to look after someone or something
Eno s'occupe bien de son mari. Eno takes good care of her husband

Se demander – to wonder –

S'opposer à – to be opposed to, to be against
Vous vous opposez à ce projet – you are against this project.
S'habiller – to get dressed, to put on clothes

Se déshabiller – to undress, to remove or take off one's clothes

Se transformer to change into

Se regarder to look at oneself

S'orienter vers la science, la littérature – to be inclined to science or literature

S'égarer – to get lost, to lose one's way, to go astray

Se tromper – to be mistaken, to make a mistake

S'informer de – to ask about, inquire about, find out

Se renseigner sur – to make enquiries, find out, get information, to ask for information

Se coucher to lie down

Se cacher to hide

Exercise 14B. 2 Put these verbs into negative. Follow examples a and b.

a. Je me brosse les dents 3 fois par jours. - Je ne me brosse pas les dents 3 fois par jour.

b. Mon fils se couche tard. - Mon fils ne se couche pas tard.

c. Vous vous occupez bien de l'enfant. -________________________________

d. Nous nous trompons de numéro. -________________________________

e. Pendant Halloween, les enfants se déguisent.____________________________

f. Tu t'éloignes du sujet. -____

g. Dans cette affaire, vous vous fiez à la chance. -____________________________

h. Les parents de Jennifer s'opposent à son mariage. -_________________________

i. Elle s'habille en princesse. -______________________________________

j. Ils se couchent avant 21 heures. -____________________________________

k. Je me déshabille au vestiaire de la piscine. -____________________________

Exercise 14B 3. Translate into French.

E.g. You are calling a wrong number – (se tromper de numéro) – Vous vous trompez de numéro.

a. My daughter brushes her teeth every morning (se brosser les dents tous les matins)

b. When do you go to bed? – Quand est-ce que__________?(se coucher)

c. Be wary of that man. -______________________________de cet homme (se méfier)

d. Go to counter 15. -______________________________(s'adresser au guichet 15)

e. At what time are we waking up tomorrow? -__________? (se réveiller)

f. I wonder where she ***is.***______________________(se demander/se trouver)

g. Each time we get dressed (s'habiller), we look at ourselves in the mirror (se regarder)__________
____

h. Find out from the information service______________________________________auprès du service d'informations (se renseigner)

Unit 15. Category 2 verbs. These are verbs ending –cer.

These verbs are conjugated like 1A verbs except 1st person plural – ***nous*** – which takes an accent on "***c***" to become "***ç***". This change is purely for phonetic reasons:

J'annonce, tu annonces ; nous annon*ç*ons; nous commen*ç*ons
Nous avan*ç*ons, vous avancez, ils avancent

Je/j'		ce
Tu	aga-	ces
Il/elle		ce
Nous		çons
Vous		cez
Ils/elles		cent

	Je/j'	***tu***	***il/elle***	***nous***	***vous***	***ils/elles***
Tense format : Radical +	***e***	***es***	***e***	***çons***	***ez***	***ent***

acquiescer	acquiesc-	j'acquiesce	acquiesces	acquiesce	acuiesçons	acquiescez	ils acquiescent
agacer	agac-						
agencer	agenc-						
amorcer	amorc-	e	es	e	çons	ez	ent
annoncer	annonc-	j'annonce	tu annonces	il annonce	n. annonçons	v. annoncez	ils annoncent
autofinancer	autofinanc-						
avancer	avanc-	e	es	e	çons	ez	ent
balancer	balanc-						
bercer	berc-	je berce	tu berces	il berce	n. berçons	v. bercez	ils bercent
cadencer	cadenc-						
carencer	carenc-						
coincer	coinc-						
commencer	commenc-	je commence	tu commences	il commence	n. commençons	v. commencez	ils commencent
commercer	commerc-						
concurrencer	concurrenc-						
contrebalancer	contrebalanc-						
courroucer	courrouc-						
décoincer	décoinc-						
décontenancer	décontenanc-						
dédicacer	dédicac-						
Défoncer	défonc-						
déglacer	déglac-						
délacer	délac-						

dénoncer	dénonc-						
déplacer	déplac-	je déplace	tu déplaces	il déplace	n. déplaçons	v. déplacez	ils déplacent
désarmorcer	désarmorc-						
dévancer	dévanc-						
distancer	distanc-						
divorcer	divorc-	e	es	e	çons	ez	ent
effacer	effac-						
lancer	lanc-						
renforcer	renforc-						

Exercise 15.1

With the aid of the presentation on Category 2 conjugation table below, supply the endings corresponding to the subject pronouns or nouns. Always use "çons" for nous – that is 1st person plural.

acquiescer	acquies-						
agacer	aga-						
agencer	agen-						
amorcer	amor-	ce	ces	ce	çons	cez	cent
annoncer	annon-	j'annonce	tu annonces	il annonce	n. annonçons	v. annoncez	ils annoncent
autofinancer	autofinan-						
avancer	avan-	ce	ces	ce	çons	cez	cent

a. Nous___________toujours à 8h00 (commencer), et nous terminons à 17h00.

b. Vous_________________le début du programme. (annoncer)

c. J'___________toujours les anciens messages de mon portable. (effacer)

d. Est-ce que toi, aussi, tu___________les anciens messages de ton portable? (effacer)

e. Ils__________un nouveau logiciel très puissant (lancer)

f. L'usine___________son effectif (staff strength) (renforcer).

g. Je________________ma voiture, sinon je risque une amende. (déplacer)

h. Nous___________lentement mais sûrement. (avancer)

Exercise 15.2 Supply the endings of the verbs in the present tense

a. Chaque fois que nous termin___________, la maîtresse effac____le tableau noir (terminer/effacer)

b. La comédienne publi______la naissance de son enfant sur Facebook : « C'est avec grand plaisir que nous annon______la naissance de notre fils » (publier/annoncer)

c. Plusieurs joueurs renonc______aux championnats de leurs clubs pour jouer avec leurs équipes nationales. (renoncer).

d. La police lanc________un appel aux témoins pour élucider le crime (lancer)

e. Quand il me regard_____, j'ai l'impression que son regard me transperc___________ (regarder/transpercer).

f. Dommage ! Ils divorc______après plusieurs années de mariage. Mais Jacky affirm_______ que son mari la forc___depuis des années. (divorcer/affirmer/forcer)

g. James, n'oubli_____pas que c'est en toi que nous pla_____nos espoirs. (oublier/placer)

h. Où est-ce que vous plac___votre argent ? Nous, on plac___le nôtre en fonds immobiliers. (placer)

i. Ne forc___pas la porte. Demand___si le concierge a un double de clé. (forcer/demander)

j. Tu risqu_____une amende si tu ne déplac_____pas ta voiture après 1 heure. (risquer/déplacer)

k. Depuis des mois maintenant, les candidats lanc____leurs campagnes électorales les uns après les autres. (lancer)

l. Nous tra______les routes, nous per_________les montagnes (tracer/percer).

m. Combien d'agents de sécurité plac______-vous ici le week-end ? (placer)

Exercise 15.3 Put these sentences into negative, according to the example below.

E.g. Le président annonce son avenir politique ce soir. – Le président n'annonce pas son avenir politique ce soir

a. On remplace l'équipe qui gagne. -____

b. Vous divorcez après 30 ans de mariage. -____________________________________

c. Les hommes renoncent au congé de paternité. -_______________________________

d. Nous avançons dans ce bouchon. -____

e. L'entreprise force ses employés à travailler le dimanche.______________________

f. Les discussions avancent bien. -______________________

g. Mon travail avance à ma satisfaction. -______________________

h. Ils placent leur argent dans l'immobilier.______________________

i. Mais tu agaces mes copines. -______________________

j. Monsieur le maire, vous exercez vos fonctions très bien.-______________________

k. Nous exerçons nos esprits. Sinon, ils deviennent inactifs.______________________

l. On remplace un attaquant par un défenseur.______________________

m. Elle exerce une grande influence sur ses collègues. -______________________

n. J'avance avec mon temps

o. Nous plaçons des militaires dans ces zones. -______________________

Unit 16. Category 3A verbs. Present tense. These verbs end in –ger

		Je/j'	*Tu*	*Il/elle*	*Nous*	*Vous*	*Ils/elles*
		e	*es*	*e*	*eons*	*ez*	*ent*
abroger	abrog-						
adjuger	adjug-						
affliger	afflig-	j'afflige	tu affliges	il afflige	affligeons	affligez	affligent
allonger	allong-						
aménager	aménag						
arranger	arrang-						
asperger	asperg-						
avantager	avantag-						
bouger	boug-	*e*	*es*	*e*	*eons*	*ez*	*ent*
bridger	bridg-						
centrifuger	centrifug-						
changer	chang-						
charger	charg-						
colliger	collig-						
converger	converg-						
corriger	corrig-	je corrige	tu corriges	il corrige	n. corrigeons	v. corrigez	ils corrigent
décharger	décharg-						
décourager	décourag-						
dédommager	dédommag-						
dégager	dégag-						

Je		e
Tu	chang-	es
Il/elle		e
Nous		eons
Vous		ez
Ils/elles		ent

Exercise 16.1

Conjugate these verbs as in the table below. First, create the radical of each verb; then add the endings corresponding to the pronouns.

Je/j'	***Tu***	***Il/elle***	***Nous***	***Vous***	***Ils/elles***
e	***es***	***e***	***eons***	***ez***	***ent***

Engager, dégager, changer, déménager, encourager, ranger, arranger, décourager.

Note that ***nous = -geons (for "–ger" verbs)***

Exercise 16.2 Provide the appropriate forms of these verbs in present tense

a. La crise_________________nos priorités (changer)

b. S'il vous plaît, quel est le taux de change. – Combien_____________-vous ? (changer)

c. Nous ne_____________pas assez de fruits et légumes. (manger)

d. Tu_________________trop, Kemi. Arrête de bouger maintenant. (bouger)

e. Christie_____________sa chambre chaque matin avant d'aller à l'école. (ranger)

f. Nous ne________________pas en cas d'exploitation des enfants. (transiger)

g. Est-ce que vous__________en première classe ? (voyager)

h. Je ne_____________pas en première classe. (voyager)

i. La panne d'électricité______le stade dans l'obscurité. (plonger)

j. Je_________________dans le bonheur depuis que j'ai rencontré ma copine. (nager)

k. Eveline___________________une chambre avec une autre étudiante. (partager)

l. Les locataires______________la cuisine, les toilettes et les douches (partager)

m. Aujourd'hui, les femmes___________des entreprises et des pays aussi bien que les hommes. (diriger)

n. Tu_______________bien les ingrédients, s'il te plaît. (mélanger).

Exercise 16.3 Answer in the negative as in the example below

Est-ce que vous arrangez un entretien avec le président?
Non, je n'arrange pas d'entretien avec lui.

a. Est-ce que ces événements ***présagent*** la fin du monde ? – Non, ils________________________
____

b. Est-ce que vous ***exigez*** le départ du président ? – Non, nous____________________________ son départ.

c. À peine arrivé, est-ce que tu envisages de changer de club ?
– Non, je__________________________de club, je demande qu'on respecte le contrat.

d. Est-ce qu'ils ***déménagent*** bientôt ? – Non, ils____

e. Est-ce qu'elle ***range*** ses affaires avant de rentrer à la maison? – Non, elle__________________

f. Est-ce que tu ***bouges*** beaucoup en ce moment ? – Non, je______________________________

g. Est-ce que les prix des smartphones ***bougent*** en ce moment ? – Non, ils__________________

h. ***Envisagez***-vous de déménager? – Non, nous____

i. Est-ce que le coach ***prolonge*** son contrat avec Super Falcon?
– Non, il____

j. Est-ce que l'entreprise ***engage***) du personnel en ce moment ?
Non, elle____

Unit 17. Exprimez autrement: saying it differently – Ne … verb…. que means only, and can be used to replace the adverb seulement.

You can combine the expression with any verb of your choice. Place the verb between "***ne***" and "***que***":
Je bois seulement du chocolat chaud – je ne ***bois*** que du chocolat chaud.

Je travaille seulement 3 jours par semaine. – Je **ne *travaille* que** 3 jours par semaine.
I work only 3 days a week.

Il est président seulement depuis 2 ans. – Il ***n'est*** président ***que*** depuis 2 ans.
He has been president for only 2 years.

Elle a seulement 10 ans. – Elle ***n'a que*** 10 ans.
She is only 10 years old.

Pour rester minces, nous mangeons ***seulement*** 2 fois par jour.

Pour rester minces, nous ***ne mangeons que*** 2 fois par jour. – To stay slim, we eat only twice a day.
Ils gagnent ***seulement*** N25'000 par mois. – Ils ***ne gagnent que*** N25'000 par mois.
They earn only N25'000 per month.

Exercise 17.1 Re-write these sentences following the example below.

Jane travaille seulement le lundi et le mercredi. – Jane ne travaille que le lundi et le mercredi.

J'ai seulement un vélo-moto. – Je n'ai qu'un vélomoteur.

a. Nous voyageons seulement trois fois par an.____________________

b. Je surfe seulement 1 heure par jour sur le net.____________________

c. Ils sortent ensemble seulement depuis 3 mois. -____________________

d. Vous fumez seulement 10 cigarettes par jour. -____________________

e. Elle a seulement 15 élèves cette année. -____________________

f. Nous avons seulement 3 semaines de vacances par an. -____________________

g. Les jumelles ont seulement 17 ans. -____________________

h. La séance commence seulement à partir de 18 heures. -____________________

i. Il se déplace seulement avec ses gardes de corps. -____________________

j. Cela arrive seulement une fois dans la vie. -____________________

Unit 18. Adjectives: the comparative and superlative forms

Michael est un grand garçon. – Michael is a tall boy.

Ibe est ***plus grand que*** Michael. – Ibe is ***taller than*** Michael.

John est ***le plus grand*** des trois garçons. John is the tallest of the three boys.

Catherine est une grand***e*** fille. - Catherine is a tall girl.
Anna est ***plus grande que*** Catherine. - Anna is taller than Catherine

Christie est ***la plus grande fille de*** la classe. Christie is the tallest girl in the class.

Grand(e), plus grand(e), le/la plus grand(e) = tall, taller, tallest

John est un beau garçon (a handsome boy).
Pascal est ***plus beau que*** John. Pascal is more handsome than John,
Patrick est ***le plus beau garçon de l'école.*** – the most handsome boy in the school.

Beau, plus beau, le plus beau = handsome, more handsome, most handsome

Belle, plus belle, la plus belle = beautiful, more beautiful most beautiful

<u>The Comparative degree</u>: compare two objects or persons using: ***plus + adj + que***:

plus beau que – more handsome than; plus sage que – wiser than

Frank est ***plus sage que*** Carlos. Frank is wiser than Carlos

Anita est ***plus belle que*** Rosa. Anita is prettier than Rosa

Jane est ***plus jeune que*** Ada – Jane is younger than Ada

The Superlative degree: ***le/la/les plus + adj***:

Yussuf est le plus sage de son village. – Yussuf is the wisest man in his village

Yemisi est la plus sage de sa famille. – Yemisi is the wisest in her family.

Sarah est la plus belle fille de sa classe. – Sarah is the prettiest girl in her class

Use ***le/la/les*** depending on the gender/number of the person(s) or the thing(s)

Richard est un homme pauvre (a poor man). Martin est ***plus pauvre que*** Martin (poorer than Martin).

Leo est l'homme ***le plus pauvre*** du quartier. Leo is ***the poorest*** man in the area.

Warren Buffet est un homme d'affaires très riche. – Warren is a very rich businessman.

Bill Gates est ***plus riche que*** Buffet. – Bill Gates richer than W. Buffet

Carlos Slim est actuellement l'homme ***le plus riche*** du monde. – Carlos Slim is currenty the ***richest man in the world.***
Dangote est l'homme ***le plus riche*** d'Afrique. – Dangote is the richest man in Africa
Le Zambèze est un long fleuve. Le Congo est ***plus long que*** le Zambèse.

Le Nil est ***le plus long*** fleuve d'Afrique. The Nile is ***the longest*** river in Africa

ThePositive degree	***The Comparative degree***	***The Superlative degree***
Intelligent(e)	***plus intelligent***(e)	***le plus intelligent, la plus intelligente***
Intelligent	more intelligent	the most intelligent
Fiable	plus fiable	le/la plus fiable (the most reliable)
Cher/chère	plus cher/chère	le plus cher, la plus chère
Dear	dearer	the dearest
Chaud(e)	plus chaud(e)	le plus chaud, la plus chaude
Hot	hotter	the hottest.
		Le jour le plus chaud. The hottest day
Froid(e)	plus froid(e)	le plus froid, la plus froide
Cold	colder	the coldest.

L'hiver le plus froid - the coldest winter

Bon, bonne (good)	meilleur(e) (better)	le meilleur, la meilleure (the best)
Mauvais(e) (bad)	pire (worse)	le/la pire (the worst)
Active	plus active	la plus active /les plus actives
Passive	plus passive	la plus passive/ les plus passives

Janet est la plus active de son équipe – Janet is the most active in her team

Indicate uniform adjectives with "***U***" (same form for masculine and feminine singular), and use "***le"*** or "***la" for the superlative singular***, as the case may be. Add ***les*** to the superlative plural.

Exercise 18.1

Fill in the blanks with the comparative and superlative forms of the adjectives

Sérieux	plus sérieux	le plus sérieux (singular), les plus sérieux (plural)
Efficace	plus efficace	le/la plus efficace (the most efficient/effective) Les plus efficaces (the most efficient/effective (plural).

a.	puissant	plus puissant	le plus puissant
b.	lourde	plus lourde	la plus lourde
c.	sérieuses	plus sérieuses	les plus sérieuses
d.	sérieux	____________	____________
e.	efficace	____________	____________
f.	efficaces	____________	____________
g.	jeune	____________	____________
h.	ancienne	____________	____________
i.	ancien	____________	____________
j.	anciens	____________	____________
k.	beau	____________	____________
l.	belles	____________	____________
m.	fidèle	____________	____________
n.	fidèles	____________	____________
o.	proche	____________	____________
p.	frais	____________	____________
q.	fraîches	____________	____________
r.	précieuse	____________	____________
s.	aible	____________	____________
t.	heureux	____________	____________
u.	récieuses	____________	____________
v.	rapide	____________	____________

Exercise 18.2 Compare two persons or situations, using « plus + adjective + que"

E.g. Nike est mince (slim). Yetunde est ***plus mince que*** Nike (slimmer than Nike)
Mon équipe est ***bonne***. Mais ton équipe est ***meilleure que*** la mienne (better than....)

a. Dino est un très bon joueur. Mais Messi est______________________Dino

b. Sabina est sage. Mais Ada______________________Sabina

c. Le professeur des mathématiques est sympathique. Mais le professeur d'anglais___________
____le prof des maths.

d. Blanche Neige est un conte drôle. Mais Chaperon Rouge est un conte.
____Blanche Neige.

e. Le Rugby est un sport populaire. Mais le football est_________________Rugby.

f. Tes pneus sont fiables. Mes les miens______________________les tiens.

g. Cette erreur est grave. Mais l'autre est____________________________________

h. Une voiture est rapide. Mais un avion est_____________________une voiture.

i. La vieille dame est laide. Mais la sorcière est____________________la vieille dame.

j. L'ordinateur de Chuks est performant. Mais celui d'Osita est__________________

k. Les adultes sont rapides. Mais les jeunes sont______________________les adultes.

l. Obi est grand. Mais Mary est___________________________Obi/lui.

***Exercise 18.3 Construct interrogative sentences showing the comparative forms of the adjectives, as in the examples below*:**

Les filles sont ***précises***_______________________? (garçons)
Est-ce que les filles sont ***plus précises que*** les garçons ?

Une Mercedes est ***chère***_______________________(une Ferrari)
Est-ce qu'une Mercedes ***est plus chère qu'***une Ferrari ?

a. Les femmes sont ***prudentes*** -_____________________________ ? (les hommes)
b. La tortue est lente -_____________________________________ ? (l'escagort)
c. Le joueur est riche. -____________________________________ ? (le coach)
d. La reine est belle. -_____________________________________ ? (Blanche-Neige)
e. Les langues sont difficiles. -_____________________________ ? (les mathématiques)
f. Les autoroutes sont mauvaises. -__________________________ ? (les routes régionales)
g. La toundra est dense. -__________________________________ ? (la forêt tropicale)
h. Certaines espèces sont faibles. -___________________________ ? (les autres)
i. Les Jardins suspendus de Babylone sont anciens. -__________ ?(la Pyramide de Gizeh)

Unit 18B. Comparing quantities plus de ....que – more ... than ; moins de ... que– less than

Study these examples to learn to say ***more of a particular thing than, less... than***

E.g Ma voiture a 7 places – (My car is a 7-seater). Ta voiture en a 4. – (Yours is a 4-seater).

Ma voiture a ***plus de places que*** ta voiture. – My car has more seats than yours.

Ta voiture a ***moins de places que*** la mienne (ma voiture). – Your car has less seats than mine

Obi a 50 moutons. - Obi has 50 sheep. Madu en a 100. Madu has 100 of them

Obi a ***moins de moutons que*** Madu. – Obi has less sheep than Madu.

Madu a ***plus de moutons que*** Obi. – Madu has more sheep than Obi.

Exercise 18B Use plus de ....que (more ....than, or ***moins de ... que*** – less .... than)

1. Il y a 20 élèves dans la classe d'Ibe et 30 élèves dans celle d'Ade.
   Ade a plus d'élèves qu'Ibe. Ibe a moins d'élèves qu'Ade

2. Ma sœur a 20 paires de chaussures. J'en ai 10.
   Ma sœur a____________________de chaussures que moi. J'ai________________de chaussures que ma soeur

3. Moussa a 5 vaches. Youssouf en a 15. Youssouf a____________________que Moussa.
   Moussa a__________de vaches que Youssouf.

4. Nous avons 7 boubous. Vous en avez 12. Vous avez_______de boubous_______nous.
   Nous avons_______de boubous_______vous

5. Ibe a 6 enfants – 2 garçons et 4 filles. Ibe a_____________de garçons que de filles.
   Ibe a______ de filles que de garçons.

6. Il y a 20 femmes et 15 hommes au cabinet du président.
   Il y a______________de femmes que d'hommes au cabinet du président. Il y a_________ d'hommes__________de femmes au cabinet du président.

7. Le stade d'Uyo compte 50000 places. Celui de Lagos en compte 40000.
   Le stade de Lagos compte_________de places____________celui d'Uyo.
   Le stade d'Uyo compte__________de places___________celui de Lagos.

8. L'université de Bénin a 10000 étudiants. L'université de Zaria en a 20000.
   L'université de Zaria a_________________que l'université de Bénin.

Unit 19. Adjectives: the Comparative degree of similarity

Aussi beau que; aussi fort que; aussi riche que; aussi paresseux que; aussi faible que
As beautiful as; as strong as; as rich as; as lazy as; as weak as; ***aussi pauvre que*** – as poor as;

Biola est ***aussi belle que*** Chinyere. Biola is as beautiful as Chinyere.

Dantata est ***aussi riche que*** Henry Stephens. Dantata is as rich as Henry Stephens.

Le voyou est ***aussi malhonnête que*** son frère. The crook is as dishonest as his brother.

We use ***aussi + adjective + que*** to form the ***comparative degree of similarity***.

The ***Comparative Degree expressing inferiority***

This can be expressed in two ways: ***pas aussi fort que*** … not as strong as…
Or ***moins fort que***….less strong than.
Yemisi n'est ***pas aussi grande que*** son mari. – Yemisi is not as tall as her husband.
Yemisi est ***moins grande que*** son mari.

Dantata n'est pas aussi riche que Dangote. – Dantata is not as rich as Dangote.

Lola ***n'est pas aussi belle qu'***Amaka can also be expressed as:

Lola est ***moins belle qu'***Amaka. Lola is less beautiful than Amaka.

Dantata ***n'est pas aussi riche que*** Dangote can also be expressed as:

Dantata est ***moins riche que*** Dangote

N'est pas aussi riche que = est moins riche que – "not as rich as" means "less rich than"

Chike ***n'est pas aussi sage que*** sa sœur. – Chike is not as good or well-behaved as his sister.

Exercise 19.1 Write the sentences showing the comparative form of similarity, as in the example below

Cristiano Ronaldo est vif. Lionel Messi est vif aussi.
Lionel Messi est aussi vif que Cristiano Ronaldo. Messi is as sharp/quick as Ronaldo.

a. Les cheveux de Sandra sont longs. Ceux de Céline sont longs aussi.
   – Les cheveux de Sandra____

b. Le sac à main de Buky est lourd. Sa valise est lourde aussi.
   – Le sac à main de Buky est____

c. La voiture est rapide. Le train est rapide aussi. – La voiture__________________

d. Mon oncle est honnête. Ma tante est honnête aussi.
   -Mon oncle____

e. La directrice est élégante. L'éducatrice est aussi élégante. –
   - L'éducatrice est____________________la directrice__________________

f. Ma voiture est grande. La vôtre aussi est grande.
   - Ma voiture____

g. Ma robe est jolie. Celle de ma sœur est jolie aussi.
   – Ma robe____

Exercise 19.2 Write the sentences showing the comparative form of inferiority.

E.g. Baker ***n'est pas aussi rapide que*** Bolt – Baker ***est moins rapide que*** Bolt.

a. Ma voiture ***n'est pas aussi confortable que*** la tienne.___________________

b. Les systèmes informatiques chez-nous ne sont pas aussi performants que chez-vous.
   -____

c. Certains étudiants ne sont pas aussi brillants que les autres. -_________________

d. Tu n'es pas aussi prudent que Susan. -___________________________________

e. Dans les facs aujourd'hui, les garçons ne sont pas aussi nombreux que les filles. -__________
   ____

f. Cette vendeuse n'est pas aussi polie que ses collègues.______________________

g. Le nouveau pilote n'est pas aussi rapide que Vettel. -_________________________

h. Ils ne sont pas aussi intelligents qu'on le croit. -___________________________

i. Le Zambèze n'est pas aussi long que le Niger. -_____________________________

Unit 20. Adjectives: the superlative form

The superlative form of adjectives is constructed as follows:

Superlative = le, la *or* ***les + plus + adj***, depending on whether the adjective is masculine, feminine, singular or plural.

Le Nil est ***le plus long*** fleuve de l'Afrique. The Nile is the longest river in Africa.

Le Ghana est le pays ***le plus stable*** de l'Afrique de l'ouest. – Ghana is the most stable country in West Africa.

Ronke est ***la plus jeune*** étudiante de sa classe. – Ronke is the youngest student in her class.
L'Arabie saoudite est ***le plus grand*** producteur de pétrole du monde.

Roger Federer est ***le meilleur*** joueur de tennis de tous les temps. Roger Federer is the best tennis player of all time.

Bon, meilleur, le meilleur.(masc/singular) – good better the best
Bonne, meilleure, la meilleure (fem/singular) – good, better, the best.

Voici ***le meilleur*** athlèthe de l'année ; la meilleure comédienne de Nollywood.

le meilleur footballeur, ***le meilleur*** acteur, ***le meilleur*** chanteur (masc/sing)
la meilleure joueuse, ***la meilleure*** actrice, ***la meilleure*** chanteuse (fem/sing)

les meilleurs films de l'année – the best films of the year. (masc/pl)
Voici ***les 10 meilleures*** comédies de cette année. (fem/pl)

Mauvais(e), pire, le pire, la pire- bad worse the worst.

Qui est ***le pire*** élève de la classe? - Who is the worst pupil in the class?
Voici ***la pire*** comédie de 2016. This is the worst comedy/play of 2016.

Quels sont les moyens ***les plus sûrs*** pour avancer dans la vie ?
Quelles sont les méthodes ***les plus sûres*** pour apprendre une langue ?

Exercise 20.1 Complete the sentences with the superlative forms of the adjectives in italics.

La police vient d'arrêter le criminel *dangereux* du pays. La police vient d'arrêter le criminel ***le plus dangereux*** du pays.

a. Les victimes racontent les moments________________*difficiles* aux mains des ravisseurs.

b. Cette victoire est le______________________*bel* exploit sportif dans notre région.

c. Le__________*bel* homme n'est pas forcément le__________*riche.*

d. Voici les portes_________________*étroites.*

e. Le lion est probablement la bête_________________*féroce.*

f. Nous sommes le jour_____________*long* de l'année.

g. Les_________*belles* femmes du monde ne sont pas forcément celles dont on lit dans les média.

h. La critique la________*virulente* vient, bien entendu, de l'opposition.

i. Le Kilimandjaro est la____________*haute* montagne d'Afrique.

j. X est élu le *bon* sportif et Y la *bonne* sportive de l'année.

Exercise 20.2 Continuation of the same exercise

a. Nous cherchons les épiceries les moins *chères.*

b. Manchester United et FC Barcelona sont parmi les clubs__________*riches* du monde.

c. *L'important*, c'est d'être en bonne santé.

d. C'est la *mauvaise* performance du club.

e. Jaqueline atteint l'endroit______________________*profond* du lac.

f. Ma grand-mère est la____________________*vieille* femme de mon village.

g. Parmi les délégués, il y a le_____________________*haut* fonctionnaire de l'état.

h. Le________________*grand* problème, c'est le manque d'accès aux informations.

i. C'est le___________________*beau* cadeau d'anniversaire que j'aie jamais reçu.

j. Nous avons passé les (*bonnes)*_____________vacances avec les moyens_______________*modestes.*

k. Lagos est____________________________*grande* ville du Nigeria.

l. Jane dit qu'elle est la maman__________________*heureuse.*

m. C'est la_________________pizza que j'aie jamais mangé. (*mauvaise)*

Unit 21. The Ordinal superlatives.

While cardinal number is used to express quantity, ordinal superlative is used to show the ***order, position or rank*** of a person or a thing.

L'Arabie saoudite est le plus grand producteur mondial de pétrole. L'Arabie saoudite est le ***premier*** (1er) pays producteur de pétrole. Saudi Arabia is the world's biggest oil producer, or the first oil producer.

La Russie est le ***deuxième*** (2ème) plus grand producteur mondial de pétrole. Russia is the 2nd biggest oil producer in the world.

Les Etat-Unis sont le ***troisième*** (3rd) plus grand producteur de pétrole. The USA is the third biggest oil producer.

L'Iran est le ***quatrième*** (4ème) plus grand producteur de pétrole du monde.

Le Nigeria est le ***douzième*** (12ème) plus grand producteur de pétrole du monde. Nigeria is the 12th biggest oil producer in the world

Exercise 21.1 Write the ordinal superlative, as in the examples below:

La liste FIFA des meilleurs buteurs de tous les temps – Fifa's list of all time best goal-scorers.

Messi = 91 buts ; Müller = 86 buts; Pelé = 75 buts
Messi est *le meilleur* buteur avec 91 buts en une saison.
Messi is the highest goal-scorer with 91 goals in one season

Muller est *le deuxième meilleur* buteur avec 86 buts – Muller is the second highest scorer with 86 goals. goals; Pelé est le troisième meilleur buteur avec 75 buts. – Pelé is the third highest goal-scorer with 75 goals.

A. ***Voici les 6 plus longs fleuves (the longest rivers) d'Afrique*** :
1. Le Nil 2. Le Niger 3. Le Congo 4. Le Sénégal 5. L'Orange 6. Le Zambèze.

Write the ordinal number of the superlatives using the above patterns.

E.g. Le Nil est le plus long fleuve d'Afrique. Le Niger est le deuxième plus long fleuve d'Afrique.

Le Congo est le________________plus long fleuve d'Afrique.

Le Sénégal est________________plus long fleuve d'Afrique.

L'Orange est le______plus long fleuve d'Afrique. Le Zambèze est le__________plus long fleuve.

B. Voici la liste des 4 ***meilleures*** joueuses de tennis du monde :

1. Serena Williams 2. Angelique Kerber 3.Simona Halep. 4. Petra Kvitova

1. Williams est actuellement la meilleure joueuse du monde. Elle occupe la première place de la WTA.

2. Angelique Kerber est ***la deuxième meilleure joueuse*** mondiale. Elle occupe la ________________________________ place de la WTA.

3. Radwanska est la ____

4. Simona Halep est la ____

C. Voici la liste des 5 plus riches Nigérians: 1. Dangote. 2. Mabo 3. Kedu. 4 Oghenovo 5. Abadie

1. Dangote est le plus riche Nigérian.

2. Mabo est le deuxième plus riche Nigérian.

3. Kedu est le____________________Nigérian.

4. Le______________plus riche Nigérian s'appelle Oghenovo.

5. Le_____________________plus riche Nigérian s'appelle Abadie.

D. Voici la liste de nos comédiennes les plus ***célèbres***:

1. La plus célèbre comédienne s'appelle Kachi

2. La deuxième comédienne la plus célèbre s'appelle Obirin.

3. Yariya est la____________comédienne_________________________

4. La______________comédienne________________________est Mlle Ifo

5. La cinquième comédienne__________________________s'appelle Hajiya.

Exercise 21.2 Voici la liste des plus grands producteurs de cacao. Complete the sentences with the ordinal adjectives

1. La Côte d'Ivoire est le pays le plus grand producteur de cacao du monde. Ainsi, elle occupe la première place mondiale
2. Le Brésil est le ***deuxième*** plus grand producteur de cacao du monde.
3. L'Indonésie est le trois-_______________plus grand producteur mondial de cacao.
4. Le Ghana est le quatri-_______________plus grand producteur de cacao.
5. Le Nigéria est le cinqui-_______________plus grand producteur mondial de cacao

Exercose 21.3 1. ***Follow the example below to construct the sentences.***

Use the same pattern and place these nationals according to their order of chocolate consumption:

1. Les Suisses sont ***les plus grands consommateurs*** de chocolat. (Ils sont les premiers consommateurs de chocolat, (or) ils occupent la première place).
2. Les Autriciens sont ***les deuxièmes plus grands*** consommateurs de chocolat.
3. Les Norvégiens
4. Les Belges
5. Les Anglais

You can use ***les premiers consommateurs, les deuxièmes plus grands, les troisièmes plus grands consommateurs, les quatrièmes plus grands consommateurs, les cinquièmes plus grands.***

Exercise 21.4 Complete the following questions with the superlatives of the adjectives, as in the example.

E.g. Quels sont ***les mauvais souvenirs*** de votre enfance?
– Quels sont ***les pires souvenirs*** de votre enfance?

a. Quels sont ***les bons*** *rôles* que vous ayez joués ?

b. Selon vous, quels sont *les*____***grands*** *acteurs* et *les* ***grandes*** *actrices* de Nollywood de tous les temps ?

c. *Le*____***jeune*** de mes enfants a 10 ans. *La*____***vieille*** comédienne a 60 ans, alors que *le*__________***vieux*** comédien a 65 ans.

d. Le moment *le*_____________***difficile*** de ma carrière était tout au début.

e. Selon vous, quelles sont *les* valeurs____________***importantes*** dans la vie ?

f. La baleine (whale) est *le*__________*grand* mammifère (mammal) du monde.

Bibliography

Maïa Grégoire and Odile Thiévenaz: Grammaire Progressive du Français avec 500 exercices CLE INTERNATIONAL, 1995, Paris.

Bescherelle POCHE : Les Tableaux pour conjuguer Les règles pour accorder Tous les verbes d'usage courant HATIER, Paris, Juin 1999

LE PETIT ROBERT 1 DICTIONNAIRE ALPHABÉTIQUE ET ANALOGIQUE DE LA LANGUE FRANCAISE Paris, 1989

I am also grateful to the following publishers :

LE GRAND Robert & Collins Dictionnaire FRANÇAIS-ANGLAIS /ANGLAIS –FRANÇAIS

HarperCollins Publishers, 2007, Glasgow G64 2QT, Great Britain.

The AMERICAN HERITAGE dictionary of THE ENGLISH LANGUAGE, 3RD EDITION, 1992 Boston, MA 02116

About the Author

The author has a degree in Modern French Language and Literature, and a certificate of Advanced Studies in Intercultural Relations from the University of Geneva.

He taught French in secondary schools in Lagos, Nigeria, worked as a translator with the Embassy of Nigeria, Bern, Switzerland, with the Swiss Federal Office for Migration, in addition to various Swiss cantonal Administrations on Asylum matters. He currently works as an independent translator and interpreter in Switzerland.

Printed in the United States
By Bookmasters